NEW VANGUARD • 176

IMPERIAL JAPANESE NAVY HEAVY CRUISERS 1941–45

MARK STILLE   ILLUSTRATED BY PAUL WRIGHT

First published in Great Britain in 2011 by Osprey Publishing,
Midland House, West Way, Botley, Oxford, OX2 0PH, UK
44-02 23rd St, Suite 219, Long Island City, NY 11101, USA
Email: info@ospreypublishing.com

Osprey Publishing is part of the Osprey Group.

A CIP catalog record for this book is available from the British Library

ISBN: 978 1 84908 148 1
Ebook ISBN: 978 1 84908 171 9

Page layout by Melissa Orrom Swan, Oxford
Index by Mike Parkin
Typeset in Sabon and Myriad Pro
Originated by United Graphics Pte Ltd
Printed in China through Worldprint Ltd

11 12 13 14 15   11 10 9 8 7 6 5 4 3 2

The Woodland Trust
Osprey Publishing is supporting the Woodland Trust, the UK's leading
woodland conservation charity, by funding the dedication of trees.

www.ospreypublishing.com

ACKNOWLEDGMENTS

The author is indebted to Jonathan Parshall and Keith Allen who graciously
reviewed the text and clarified many points. The author would also like to
thank the staffs of the Naval History and Heritage Command Photographic
Section and the Yamato Museum, and Tohru Kizu, editor of the *Ships of
the World* magazine, for their assistance in procuring photographs used
in the book.

CONTENTS

IMPERIAL JAPANESE NAVY HEAVY CRUISERS 1941–45

INTRODUCTION

The heavy cruiser force of the Imperial Japanese Navy (IJN) was demonstrably one of its most successful components during the Pacific War. By 1941, the Japanese had fielded 18 heavy cruisers, putting them on numerical parity with the US Navy. Japanese cruisers entered the war with a reputation for superior size and firepower compared to their American and British counterparts, suspected by many to be the result of breaking treaty limits in place between the wars. The exploits of the IJN's heavy cruisers during the first part of the war confirmed the positive pre-war expectations of the Japanese and made them feared opponents by the Allies. While the Japanese retained the bulk of their battleships in home waters during the early and middle part of the war, their heavy cruisers spearheaded Japanese expansion into the Dutch East Indies. When the Japanese were forced onto the defensive in mid-1942, heavy cruisers again provided the backbone for their resistance in the Solomons for the rest of the year. After a comparatively quiet 1943, during which no cruisers were lost, 1944 marked the effective end of the IJN's heavy cruiser force. By the end of the war, only two heavy cruisers remained afloat, both in a damaged condition. This book tells the story of the 18 Japanese heavy cruisers that saw service in World War II.

JAPANESE NAVAL STRATEGY AND THE ROLE OF THE HEAVY CRUISER

The basic strategy of the IJN was defensive up until 1939. As the Japanese fleet was outnumbered by the US Navy, the IJN intended to let the Americans cross the Pacific before mounting a decisive action in the Western Pacific. Integral to this plan was progressive attrition of the advancing Americans by submarines and destroyers. As the US Navy approached the area of decisive battle, the Second Fleet, composed of the majority of the IJN's heavy cruisers and two squadrons of large destroyers, would come into play to inflict further destruction.

Of course, the decisive surface battle in the Western Pacific was never fought. Yet the IJN's heavy cruiser force still played an important role during the war. Since the Japanese withheld the bulk of their battleships in anticipation of a possible decisive clash, the heavy cruisers were very active during the period of Japanese expansion and provided cover for every important landing up through May 1942. When the Japanese were forced onto the defensive, and the Solomon Islands became the scene of a series of night actions, the heavy

cruisers were employed in their anticipated pre-war role of leading surface action groups in night attacks against American forces.

After 1934, the heavy cruisers were seen as the IJN's principal night-fighting unit. Under the revised Night Battle Tactics of that year, the heavy cruisers were intended primarily as a component of the Night Battle Force to attack the US battle fleet with its long-range torpedoes, inflicting heavy attrition before the Japanese battleships closed for a climactic daylight gunnery action. The *Takao* class heavy cruisers were to combine with the four *Kongo* class fast battleships to open a way through the defensive ring of the US battle fleet. Supporting the attack, and slated to deliver massed torpedo fire, were four night battle groups, each comprised of a cruiser squadron formed around a class of heavy cruiser and a destroyer squadron of 14–16 ships led by a light cruiser. This concept was modified just before the start of the war so that two battle groups attacked each side of the US battle fleet. While the massive fleet engagement desired and planned for by the Japanese never happened, this concentration on small-unit tactics paid off handsomely for the Japanese, as shown by the success of cruiser and destroyer units during the first part of the war.

To accomplish their wartime role, Japanese heavy cruisers emphasized firepower. They were designed to carry a superior gun armament compared to their likely American opponents, but the key to Japanese cruiser doctrine was the provision of a heavy torpedo armament. After much work, the Japanese developed a long-range, oxygen-propelled torpedo that came into service in 1936. These top-secret weapons were first fitted on the heavy cruisers (and later to destroyers), and gave them the capability to strike at extended range before the enemy even knew he was under attack.

5

JAPANESE HEAVY CRUISER DEVELOPMENT

Classification of Japanese heavy cruisers

Japanese heavy cruisers were known by several terms before finally settling on "heavy cruiser". The 1898 Warship and Torpedo Boat Classification Criteria called for a ship of greater than 7,000 tons designed displacement to be considered a first-rate cruiser. Officially, they were also called "A Class" cruisers and unofficially they were also called "large-model cruisers". By World War II, however, the Japanese had settled on "heavy cruiser" (*junyokan*), bringing them in line with the rest of the world's navies.

From the period of 1922 up through the end of 1938, the IJN was restricted in the numbers and types of heavy cruisers it could build by a series if international naval treaties. In fact, the entire concept of a "heavy cruiser", as it came to be known, was a construct from the treaty system. The Washington Naval Treaty, signed on February 6, 1922, placed a limit on the size of cruisers (10,000 tons maximum) and a restriction of the size of the armament (no larger than 8in guns). However, while the overall tonnage of capital ships and aircraft carriers was restricted, there was no similar limit placed on cruisers. The effect was to start a treaty cruiser building spree, with the 10,000-ton limit becoming the baseline for Japanese cruiser designs.

The design of the IJN's first heavy cruisers actually pre-dated the Washington Treaty. By July 1922, the Japanese had announced plans for the construction of eight cruisers – four of the pre-treaty 7,500-ton scout cruisers and four 10,000-ton ships. The scout cruisers became the *Furutaka* and *Aoba* classes and the first class of 10,000-ton cruisers constituted the *Myoko* class. The epitome of Japanese treaty cruiser design was the follow-on to the *Myoko* class, the four-ship *Takao* class.

After an attempt to implement further overall tonnage restrictions to cruiser construction failed at the Geneva Naval Conference in 1927, the major naval powers tried again in London in 1930. This time it was agreed to place a cap on cruiser tonnage, and existing and future cruisers were broken into two types. Type A (or heavy) cruisers were defined as ships with guns greater than 6.1in and Type B (or light) cruisers were ships with guns smaller than 6.1in. The 10,000-ton maximum and 8in gun restrictions remained in effect. The London Naval Treaty, signed April 21, 1930, set the final course for the IJN's heavy cruiser force. The allotted total tonnage for Japanese Type A cruisers was 108,400 tons standard; this had already been reached by the 12 Type A cruisers in service. For Type B cruisers, the Japanese limit was 100,450 tons standard. Per treaty stipulations, the tonnage of vessels ready for replacement could be used for new construction. For the Imperial Navy, this amounted to 50,955 tons. The Japanese decided that this remaining tonnage would be used to build four 8,500-ton units before 1936, followed by another two later. These six ships were later upgraded to become heavy cruisers, thus rounding out the IJN's pre-war heavy cruiser force at 18 units.

Myoko on April 16, 1927, during her launch at the Yokosuka Navy Yard. She was the first of eight Washington Treaty cruisers launched by the IJN in the next eight years. (Naval History and Heritage Command)

Japanese Heavy Cruiser Weapons

From the start, Japanese heavy cruiser designs emphasized firepower, and it was expected that the Imperial Navy's cruisers would out-gun and out-range their foreign contemporaries.

Main battery

After a brief flirtation with 7.9in guns, the Japanese decided to upgrade existing ships and build all future ships with 8in guns. The 8in gun mounted in a twin turret was adopted in 1931. It was a respectable weapon, but was consistently plagued with a large salvo dispersion – during gunnery

trials in 1933, this was noted to be as much as 528 yards over a range of 21,100 yards. The Japanese attempted to alleviate this problem with the installation of a device in 1938 that produced a very slight delay in the firing of the two guns in a turret, a measure that reduced interference. This served to reduce dispersion to 416 yards at 21,873 yards range for the classes with ten 8in guns. Dispersion problems for the ships with only six guns were consistently less.

As the IJN was expecting to be outnumbered in any major clash with the US Navy, the Japanese placed great emphasis on out-ranging its likely opponent so as to hit first without the threat of effective response. Due to continual modernization of heavy cruiser fire-control equipment, by 1937 the engagement range for 8in guns was extended to greater than 21,873 yards. The Japanese calculated that even at this maximum battle range, their hit probability was 6 percent. This was a wildly optimistic assessment, and as will be seen later the quality of Japanese cruiser gunnery at extended ranges during the war was mediocre at best.

The IJN's heavy cruisers were designed to maximize their capabilities during night combat. To provide illumination at night, the Japanese used a combination of searchlights and star shells. The most powerful cruiser searchlight had an effective range of 6,562 yards; if two searchlights were trained on the same target, the effective range was increased to 8,749 yards. This constituted the effective range of the cruisers in night combat.

Furutaka in her original configuration, with single 7.9in guns in "semi-turrets." She was later modernized and her appearance changed to resemble that of the *Aoba* class. To the left of *Furutaka* are *Aoba* and *Kinugasa*. (Naval History and Heritage Command)

Japanese heavy cruiser main guns				
Type	Class	Max. elevation (degrees)	Max. range (yards)	Rate of fire (rpm)
50-cal Type 3 No. 2 Model C	Aoba	40	31,606	2–3
50-cal Type 3 No. 2 Model D	Myoko	40	31,606	2–3
50-cal Type 3 No. 2 Model E	Takao (less Maya)	45	32,153	2–3
50-cal Type 3 No. 2 Model E1	Maya	70*	32,153	2–3
50-cal Type 3 No. 2 Model Mogami	Mogami	45	32,153	2–3
50-cal Type 3 No. 2 Model E2	Furutaka	45	32,153	2–3
50-cal Type 3 No. 2 Model E3	Tone	45	32,153	2–3

* Maximum theoretical elevation for anti-aircraft firing only; maximum elevation against surface targets 45 degrees.

The searchlights were controlled by a searchlight control station, which was equipped with powerful binoculars. Several types of binoculars were installed on the bridge, some as large as 7in. Night-fighting prowess was also enhanced by the development of flashless powder adopted in 1938, which concealed the source of gunfire.

Chokai firing a broadside with her 8in gun battery in 1933. Despite constant practice and attention to long-range gunnery, the accuracy of Japanese cruiser gunnery at extended ranges was notable for its lack of wartime success. At closer ranges, however, the IJN's well-drilled cruiser crews were deadly. (Naval History and Heritage Command)

Torpedo armament

The biggest difference in Japanese cruiser design compared to American heavy cruisers was the inclusion of heavy torpedo armament. A heavy torpedo battery was crucial to allow the cruiser to play its leading role in night combat and gave the vessels a long-range punch not possessed by foreign rivals. There was a clear danger to mounting such weapons – if their unprotected large warheads were hit during combat, the resulting explosion could wreck vital parts of the ship. In fact, there was considerable tension between the Naval General Staff who formulated design requirements and the principal designers of the ships whether to include torpedoes at all. In the end, the Naval General Staff got its way and a heavy torpedo armament became a staple of Japanese cruiser design.

The forward two 8in turrets on a *Takao* class cruiser. These turrets were adopted in 1931 and weighed 171 tons. One of the shortcomings of Japanese heavy cruiser 8in gun turrets was their relative lack of protection, with only 25mm of armor all round. Comparable US Navy treaty cruiser turrets were provided with as much as 203mm of frontal armor. (*Ships of the World* magazine)

Heavy cruisers employed triple and quadruple torpedo mounts. In addition to a large number of torpedoes carried in the tubes (up to 16), another set of reloads was carried. Reloading was a key skill that was constantly practiced and could be executed in a matter of minutes. In 1938, the Japanese provided their cruisers with the Type 93 Model 1 Modification 2 torpedo, which had been adopted by the IJN in 1935. This remarkable weapon, later given the nickname "Long Lance" by the Allies, possessed a 1,082lb warhead and was wakeless. It could travel up to 43,746 yards at 36 knots, 35,000 yards at 40 knots, or 21,873 yards at 48 knots. Fire control for torpedo combat was provided by a director computing system located on the bridge, which was used for targets between ranges of 10,936 yards to 43,746 yards. A second director was used for ranges under 10,936 yards.

Anti-aircraft armament

The standard Japanese long-range anti-aircraft weapon during the Pacific War was the 40-cal Type 89 5in high-angle dual mount gun. This gun was mounted on all heavy cruiser classes except *Furutaka* and *Aoba* because of weight and size issues and the *Takao* class, which did not receive them before the war because of production shortages. These ships retained the older 4.7in single mounts. The most modern fire director was the Type 94, but only the *Aoba* and both ships of the *Tone* class received them before the war due to production shortages. *Maya* received it during her conversion to an anti-aircraft cruiser during the war.

The Type 89 gun was a decent design, but suffered from a relatively short maximum range. The primary problem was with the Type 91 high-angle director, which was fitted on most heavy cruisers. Adopted in 1932, the system took 11 men to operate and the manual operation was slow in both elevation and training. The system was not designed to handle high-speed targets. In 1940, the Japanese calculated that the Type 91 director could achieve a hit percentage of 0.9 percent under battle conditions, but this proved far from reality under combat conditions.

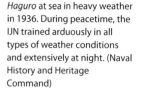

Haguro at sea in heavy weather in 1936. During peacetime, the IJN trained arduously in all types of weather conditions and extensively at night. (Naval History and Heritage Command)

Japanese heavy anti-aircraft guns		
	45-cal Type 10 4.7in	40-cal Type 89 5in
Muzzle velocity	2,706ft/sec	2,362ft/sec
Rate of fire (rpm)	10–11 max, 6–8 effective	14 max, 11–12 effective
Effective range		
Horizontal	17,060 yards	14,435 yards
Vertical	11,007 yards	8,858 yards
Effective	9,241 yards	8,092 yards
Shell weight	45.08lb	50.71lb

Light anti-aircraft armament

Before the war, the IJN decided to provide all cruisers with a standard light anti-aircraft armament of four twin Type 96 25mm mounts grouped amidships and two twin 13mm machine-guns fitted forward of the bridge. The Type 96 was destined to become the standard light anti-aircraft weapon of the IJN and was produced in single (1943), double, and triple (1941) mounts. The original twin-gun version was developed by the French firm Hotchkiss and adopted by the IJN in 1936. It was an unfortunate choice. The Type 96 twin and triple mounts possessed low training and elevating speeds, produced excessive muzzle blast, and the rate of fire was reduced by the need to keep reloading 15-round magazines. The single 25mm gun proved difficult for individual crewmen to handle.

A torpedo mount on a Japanese cruiser. The provision of torpedoes on their cruisers gave the Japanese an important advantage early in the war when they enjoyed the initiative, but when the IJN was forced onto the defensive and its cruisers subjected to increasing air attack, these weapons proved a liability and directly contributed to the loss of several ships. (*Ships of the World* magazine)

Fire control was provided by the Type 95 director, adopted in 1937, with a theoretical maximum range of 4,155 yards. The triple and double mount also had a back-up sight. The single 25mm mount and the 13mm machine guns were guided by a single open-ring sight that proved inadequate for high-speed targets. Despite the growing profusion of 25mm guns on heavy cruisers during the war, these ships grew increasingly vulnerable to air attack.

Type 96 25mm gun (1936)	
Muzzle velocity	984 yards/sec
Rate of fire (rpm)	220–240 theoretical; 110–120 actual
Anti-aircraft range	Maximum 8,200 yards; effective 766–1,633 yards
Shell weight	8.8oz

Japanese Heavy Cruiser Radar

The Japanese began to equip all their cruisers with radars from mid-1943, doing so when ships returned to Japan for repair and refit. The first set fitted was an air-search radar known formally as the Type 2 (1942) shipboard search radar Model 1 Modification 2, or abbreviated as No. 21 (2). The No. 21 (2) radar had a mattress antenna and was fitted on the top of the foremast. The radar room was located in the foremast. Another air-search radar was introduced later in 1943 and designated as the No. 13 (Type 3, No. 1, Model 3). This had a long ladder antenna and was fitted on the aft part of the foremast or the leading edge of the mainmast. The final type of cruiser radar was the No. 22 Modification 4M radar designed for surface search. This featured a twin-horn antenna design – one for transmitting and one for receiving. Units were mounted in pairs on both sides of the bridge or on the foremast. In September 1944, a fire-control version of the radar was developed and designated Modification 4S. However, this was never accurate enough to allow for true radar-controlled gunnery.

For surface targets, the No. 22 (4) could detect a battleship target at 38,276 yards, a cruiser-sized ship at 21,872 yards and a destroyer-sized target at 18,591 yards. The range error was 820–1,640ft and the bearing error up to three degrees.

Japanese heavy cruiser radars			
	No. 21 Mod. 2	**No. 13**	**No. 22 Mod. 4M**
Peak power output	5kW	10kW	2kW
Maximum range	93 miles	93 miles	37 miles
Effective Range single aircraft group of aircraft	 43 miles 62 miles	 31 miles 62 miles	 11 miles 22 miles
Accuracy	1,094–2,187 yards	2,187–3,280 yards	273–546 yards
Bearing accuracy	5–8 degrees	10 degrees	3 degrees

THE HEAVY CRUISER CLASSES

Furutaka and *Aoba* Classes
Design and construction

The Japanese were developing the 7,500-ton scout cruiser well before the Washington Treaty came into effect, though even once the treaty was ratified both their maximum displacement and gun caliber fell under treaty limits. The concept of the large scout cruiser was about producing a ship capable of performing scouting duties against the enemy's main fleet, while protecting the Japanese main fleet from enemy scouting forces. It was intended that these ships have superior capabilities to their nearest Allied counterparts of the day, the American *Omaha* class cruisers and the Royal Navy's *Hawkins* class. As was to be the pattern for all of their heavy cruisers, the Japanese aimed to put a lot on a relatively small hull. In the case of the 7,500-ton ships, it was planned that they would mount six 7.9in/50-cal single mounts and six 21in torpedo tubes. This configuration would give them a considerable firepower advantage over the American *Omaha* vessels. A high top speed of 35 knots was also required to enable the ships to keep formation with other Japanese scouting forces. To put so much on a relatively small hull would only be possible with the incorporation of many weight-saving measures. These were the responsibility of Constructor Captain (later Rear Admiral) Hiraga Yuzuru.

After construction began on the first two ships, the Naval General Staff pressured the design section to modify the design of the 7,500-ton units to fit the new 8in twin gun turrets. Work on the first two ships, *Furutaka* and *Kako*, was already too far along to accommodate such a change, but it was agreed to fit the new turrets on the next two ships, *Kinugasa* and *Aoba*. Another major modification was to fit a catapult on the last two ships, which in turn required the redesign of the aft superstructure. The redesign also incorporated an upgraded anti-aircraft fit and correction of some problems found with the smokestack and bridge of *Furutaka* and *Kako*.

The 4.7in high-angle gun was the IJN's standard treaty cruiser heavy anti-aircraft gun. It dated from 1926 and lingered on into the war on as many as eight cruisers. It weighed 10 tons. (*Ships of the World* magazine)

Furutaka **and** Aoba **class construction**				
Ship	**Built at**	**Laid down**	**Launched**	**Commissioned**
Furutaka	Nagasaki by Mitsubishi	02/05/1922	02/25/1925	03/31/1926
Kako	Kobe by Kawasaki	11/17/1922	04/10/1925	07/20/1926
Aoba	Nagasaki by Mitsubishi	02/04/1924	09/25/1926	09/20/1927
Kinugasa	Kobe by Kawasaki	01/23/1924	10/24/1926	09/30/1927

The 25mm gun was the standard light anti-aircraft weapon on all Japanese heavy cruisers. The twin mount, shown here, was introduced in 1936 and required a crew of seven to operate at full efficiency, but even fully manned it could only manage a sustained rate of fire of 110–20rpm. Despite being mounted in growing numbers on all surviving cruisers during the war, it failed to provide adequate protection against torpedo and dive-bombing attacks. (*Ships of the World* magazine)

To achieve their design speed, the 7,500-ton vessels had the highest length-to-beam ratios of any Japanese cruiser. The hull was characterized by a graceful flush upper deck with a undulating sheer line. This design and other weight-saving measures meant that the hull was only 33 percent of trial displacement for the two units of the *Furutaka* class (32 percent on *Aoba*). Propulsion was provided by four sets of turbines that produced a total of 102,000 shaft horsepower (shp). Twelve boilers located in seven boiler rooms provided the steam. As completed, all four ships either reached or exceeded their 35-knot design speed. Endurance was designed to be 7,000nm at 14 knots.

Protection was not a design emphasis. On both classes, belt and deck armor amounted to just over 12 percent of trial displacement. The main belt on the side was 76mm (running

Commissioning day for *Kako*: July 20, 1926. This exceptionally clear photo shows her initial configuration in detail. Note the two groups of six 7.9in guns arranged in a pyramid layout fore and aft. The six starboard-side fixed hull-mounted single torpedo tubes can also be made out: the first pair is located in front of the bridge and the other two are positioned in the area of the catapult. (Yamato Museum)

for 262ft of the ship's length) and the overhead protection consisted of a maximum of 35mm of steel armor on the armored deck and another 48mm of high-tensile steel on the middle deck. The forward and aft magazines were given additional protection, as were the steering gear rooms.

Overall, the protection was inadequate against 8in shells, but was judged to be sufficient to deflect 6in shells at between 13,123 and 16,404 yards' range. Underwater protection was limited to a small bulge located below the waterline at the lower edge of the main belt. This, and the internal subdivision, which featured a centerline bulkhead to limit flooding to one side of the ship, provided minimal protection against torpedoes but was comparable to foreign designs.

Armament

As designed, the *Furutaka* class mounted a main armament of six 7.9in Type 3 50-cal guns in six "semiturrets." These were of simple construction and provided minimal protection to the crews. All six were mounted on the centerline, allowing a full six-gun broadside. The Naval General Staff's push to mount the twin 7.9in turrets on the *Aoba* class resulted in a greater elevation (thus a greater maximum range) and a greater rate of fire because of the reduced physical strain on the gun crew. As originally completed, anti-aircraft armament was limited to four single 3in guns on the *Furutaka* class and four upgraded 4.7in guns on the *Aoba* class. Despite the strong objections of Hiraga, the *Furutaka* and *Aoba* classes featured fixed torpedo tubes inside the hull. Six pairs were originally fitted.

Provision of aircraft was key to the ships' role as scouting cruisers. No suitable catapult was available when design work began, so the *Furutaka* class was provided with a take-off platform for a single floatplane instead. This proved awkward, and it was easier and faster to crane the floatplane into the water and recover it in the same way. In March 1928, *Kinugasa* became the first Japanese ship to carry a catapult, soon joined by Aoba.

 FURUTAKA AND AOBA CLASSES

The top profile shows *Furutaka* in August 1942 as she appeared during the battle of Savo Island. The *Furutaka* class can be distinguished from the *Aoba* class by the different bridge, the smaller second smokestack, and, most readily, by the different positioning of the crane and catapult. Note the presence of only three 8in turrets and the single 4.7in dual-purpose guns. Both ships of the *Furutaka* class were lost in 1942 in this configuration. The second profile and overhead view depicts *Aoba* in her October 1944 configuration during the battle of Leyte Gulf. The ship retains an overall similarity to the *Furutaka* class, but many late-war modifications are evident, including the No. 21 radar in the foremast and the profusion of 25mm anti-aircraft guns.

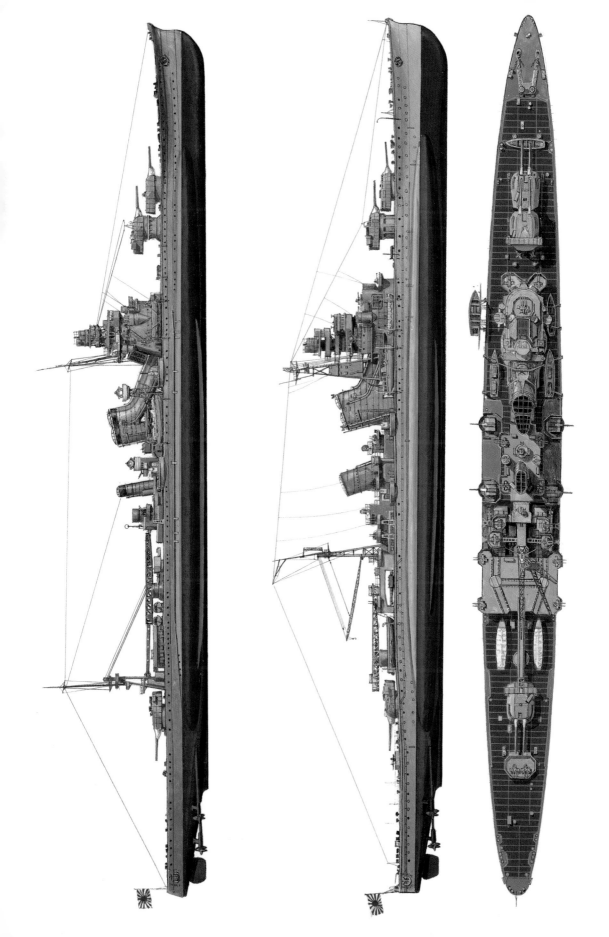

Aoba in 1928, as completed. Unlike the two *Furutakas*, the two *Aoba* class units were completed with twin 8in gun turrets. The catapult shown here was one of the first fitted to a Japanese warship. Not visible are any topside torpedo launchers, since the torpedo armament was fitted in single tubes in the hull. (Yamato Museum)

Service modifications

Being the earliest Japanese heavy cruisers, both these classes were reconstructed before the Pacific War. The first to go in for modernization were *Furutaka* and *Kako*. Their modernization occurred earlier than planned; the ships had to go into repair for engine overhauls and the Japanese used that opportunity for a complete modernization. *Kako* was modernized at Sasebo from July 1936 until December 1937 and *Furutaka* at Kure from April 1937 until April 1939. Principal work included replacing the 7.9in guns with re-bored 8in guns. The new turrets were known as E2 Model turrets, arranged as on the *Aoba* class with two forward and one aft.

The fixed torpedo tubes were replaced by two quadruple torpedo tube mounts, located one on each side. Since eight reloads were carried, each ship carried 16 torpedoes. All ships retained the 4.7in high-angle guns. Four twin Type 96 guns were fitted amidships and two twin Type 93 13mm machine guns fitted forward of the bridge.

The forward superstructure was almost totally rebuilt, which allowed for the modernization of the fire-control systems for the main, torpedo, and anti-aircraft batteries. A heavier catapult was also fitted. These improvements added another 562 tons of weight. To compensate, the beam was increased by adding larger anti-torpedo bulges filled with watertight steel tubes to increase buoyancy. The fitting of the bulges increased stability and actually reduced draft despite the additional weight from the modernization. Speed was slightly reduced to 33 knots with the increase in weight being compensated for by the replacement of the original 12 boilers with ten oil-fired *Kampon* boilers. This increased horsepower to 110,000shp. Effective endurance was increased to 7,900nm at 14 knots by the addition of greater fuel storage.

Modernization of the *Aoba* class was very similar. Both ships underwent work at Sasebo, *Kinugasa* beginning in October 1938 and *Aoba* in November 1938; both returned to service in October 1940. When completed, the two

Kinugasa as completed in 1928. The single 4.7in high-angle guns are visible (covered in canvas) and the fixed torpedo tubes can be seen below the bridge and abaft the mainmast. No catapult has been fitted yet. (Yamato Museum)

This overhead view shows *Kako* in 1941 in her wartime configuration. The single 7.9in semi-turrets have been replaced by twin 8in gun turrets, one of which can be seen aft. Four 4.7in high-angle guns are visible in the area of the smokestacks. Situated abaft the rear smokestack are the two quadruple torpedo launchers. The armored box in front of the launchers is for the torpedo reloads. The small aircraft handling area was located forward of the mainmast; the two aircraft are Type 94 reconnaissance seaplanes (Allied codename "Alf"). (Yamato Museum)

classes presented a similar appearance, with the only obvious differences being in the bridge appearance and the arrangement of the crane and catapult.

After the start of the war, three of the four ships of these classes were sunk before further modification. However, *Aoba* was considerably modified during her career. Damage in October 1942 included destruction of her No. 3 turret, which was removed and then plated over. A 25mm triple gun mount was temporarily fitted in its place. In August 1943, *Aoba* returned to Kure for major repairs. The No. 3 turret was replaced, two additional 25mm triple mounts were fitted, and a No. 21 radar was fitted. Damage to the engines, however, meant a permanent speed reduction to 28 knots.

In July 1944, *Aoba* received four triple and 15 single 25mm guns at Singapore; this gave the ship a total of 42 25mm barrels. Before the battle of Leyte Gulf, the ship carried a No. 13 and No. 22 radar. The ship's final anti-aircraft component, following a refit in June 1945, was five triple, ten double and 15 single 25mm guns.

Japanese heavy cruiser names

Based on 1905 directions from the Navy Minister, first-class cruisers were named after mountains. Second-class (eventually light) cruisers were named after rivers or streams.

Ashigara – named after a mountain in Kanagawa Prefecture
Atago – named after a mountain near Kyoto
Chikuma – named after a stream in Nagano Prefecture
Chokai – named after a mountain in Yamagata Prefecture
Furutaka – named after Mount Furutaka, located on the island of Etajima near Hiroshima
Haguro – named after a mountain in Yamagata Prefecture in northwest Honshu
Kako – named after a river in Hyogo Prefecture (confusion was caused by the fact that the name had originally been allocated to a 5,500-ton light cruiser)
Kinugasa – named after Mount Kinugasa near Kyoto
Kumano – named after a river in Mie Prefecture in Honshu
Maya – named after a mountain in Hyogo Prefecture
Mikuma – named after a river in Oita Prefecture in northeast Kyushu
Mogami – named after a stream in Yamagata Prefecture
Myoko – named after a mountain in Niigata Prefecture
Nachi – named after a mountain in Wakayama Prefecture
Suzuya – named after a stream in southern Sakhalin
Takao – named after a mountain near Kyoto
Tone – named after a river on the Kanto Plain

Wartime service

In November 1941, the four ships of the *Furutaka* and *Aoba* classes composed *Sentai* 6 (literally Division 6 in Japanese, but referring to a cruiser division) under Rear Admiral Goto Aritomo. Their first action was covering the successful invasion of Guam on December 1941. *Sentai* 6 then proceeded to cover the second Japanese attempt to invade Wake Island. Under cover of two of the Pearl Harbor carriers, Wake was successfully invaded on December 23. *Sentai* 6 was then dispatched to cover the invasion of Rabaul and Kavieng on January 23, 1942, and remained assigned to the Fourth Fleet (South Sea Force). In March 1942, the ships covered the invasion of Lae and Salamaua on New Guinea.

The next operation, the attempt to seize Port Moresby on New Guinea, did not go as well for the Japanese. *Sentai* 6 departed Truk on April 30 as part of the Main Body escorting the light carrier *Shoho*. After providing distant cover for the seizure of Tulagi in the Solomons on May 3, they again joined with *Shoho*. On May 7, 93 US carrier aircraft attacked *Shoho*, sinking her under a barrage of torpedoes and bombs. The Port Moresby operation failed and marked the first strategic Japanese setback of the war.

Sentai 6 remained in the South Pacific and was assigned to the newly created Eighth Fleet based at Rabaul. On August 7, the four cruisers departed Rabaul and headed toward Guadalcanal, where the local garrison had reported that the Americans had just landed. *Sentai* 6, along with fleet flagship *Chokai*, attacked the warships covering the American landing force and put on perhaps the best Japanese display of naval gunnery during the entire war. The battle of Savo Island on August 9 resulted in the destruction of four Allied heavy cruisers (three American and one Australian). Engaging the surprised Americans at fairly close range – 5,500 yards and less – and assisted by searchlights, star shells, and flares from the Japanese ships' aircraft, gunnery results were very good, in excess of 10 percent hits. In exchange, *Kinugasa* was hit twice and *Aoba* once, but damage was not significant. The Americans extracted a measure of revenge when, on August 10, en route to Kavieng, submarine *S-44* fired four torpedoes at *Kako*; three hit and the cruiser blew up and sank.

The next major surface engagement off Guadalcanal occurred in October 1942. Known as the battle of Cape Esperance, it was the first Japanese defeat in a night action during the war. The Japanese force was built around the three surviving cruisers of *Sentai* 6. Against an American cruiser force with the advantage of radar, Admiral Goto was slow to react. His flagship, *Aoba*, was hit by 24 shells and heavily damaged and the admiral killed. *Furutaka* was hit by a large number of shells (up to 90) and a torpedo; additionally, some of her torpedoes exploded, starting additional fires. She sank on October 12 with 33 killed. Of the 225 missing, 115 were taken prisoner. *Kinugasa* was the only bright spot for the Japanese. She hit the US cruiser *Boise* with eight shells, including one that pierced the ship below the waterline and exploded in the

forward magazine. The resulting fire would have destroyed the ship had not the water pouring through the hole made by the shell put out the fire. *Kinugasa* also hit the heavy cruiser *Salt Lake City* twice, but damage was slight.

Nachi in November 1928 showing the initial configuration of her class. The ship was actually rushed to completion to participate in the Emperor's Coronation Naval Review in December 1928. At this point she had an undisturbed sheer hull line with no catapults or superstructure abaft the mainmast. The three port-side 4.7in high-angle guns can be seen and the doors for the six port-side fixed hull-mounted torpedo tubes are just visible in the area where the catapult will be fitted. (Yamato Museum)

Now only *Kinugasa* remained operational from *Sentai 6*. On October 15, she and *Chokai* bombarded Henderson Field on Guadalcanal with 752 8in shells. On November 14, after covering another cruiser bombardment of Henderson, *Kinugasa* was attacked by dive-bombers from the carrier USS *Enterprise*. A bomb hit on the forward part of the bridge, penetrated below the waterline, and caused heavy flooding. The flooding could not be contained and the ship was eventually abandoned with the loss of 51 crewmen.

After Cape Esperance, *Aoba* was sent to Kure for repairs. The No. 3 turret was destroyed, so it was removed and the deck plated over and the ship sent back into action. On April 3, 1943, the ship was attacked by B-17 bombers at anchorage at Kavieng and was heavily damaged by a bomb and by the explosion of two of her torpedoes. The ship was beached, and later towed to Truk for repairs before returning to Japan.

Aoba was now a second-rate unit and was assigned to the First Southern Expeditionary Fleet. On March 1, 1944, the ship entered the Indian Ocean on a commerce raid with the cruisers *Tone* and *Chikuma*. Results were meager.

As part of the IJN's all-out effort during the battle for Leyte Gulf in October 1944, *Aoba* was tasked with escorting troop reinforcements to Leyte. On October 23, she was torpedoed en route to Manila by the submarine *Bream*, a single torpedo hitting her engine room. *Aoba* nevertheless departed the Philippines in November and reached Japan in December, where the damage was deemed irreparable. On March 19, at Kure, American carrier aircraft raided the base and heavily damaged *Aoba* once more. In June, the ship was moored as a floating battery near Kure, where an additional carrier raid on July 24 hit *Aoba* with a bomb, which combined with a near miss caused flooding and a starboard list. The ship settled in 25ft of water. Days later, on 28 July, the hulk was hit by another four bombs from B-24s and carrier aircraft, starting fires and breaking off the stern.

Furutaka/Aoba classes specifications (after reconstruction)	
Displacement:	11,273/11,660 tons (full load)
Dimensions:	length 607ft 6in overall; beam 55ft 6in/57ft 8in; draft 33ft
Speed:	33–34 knots
Range:	7,900/8,223nm at 14 knots
Crew:	*Furutaka* class: 50 officers and 589 enlisted; *Kinugasa*: 50 officers and 607 enlisted; *Aoba*: 54 officers and 626 enlisted since she was fitted to be squadron flagship

Myoko Class
Design and construction
The four units of what became the *Myoko* class were authorized by the Japanese Diet in March 1923. With the Washington Treaty in effect, these were the first Japanese cruisers designed under the treaty restrictions. The designers

of the class, led by Hiraga, had a difficult time achieving the requirements of the Naval General Staff on the allowed 10,000-ton displacement. The original design requirements called for a ship mounting eight 8in guns in four turrets, a torpedo armament of eight 24in torpedo tubes in fixed mounts below the upper deck, protection against 6in shells with vital areas protected against indirect fire by 8in shells, a speed of more than 35 knots, and a radius of 10,000nm at 13.5 knots. Hiraga convinced the Naval General Staff to add another 8in turret, which would enable the ship to out-gun its foreign opponents, and most importantly to eliminate the torpedo armament, since the fixed tubes were actually located over the engine rooms and the detonation of a torpedo warhead could cause crippling damage. Hiraga's modified design, approved in August 1923, adhered to the treaty tonnage limit and did not include torpedo tubes. However, the Naval General Staff was not easily dissuaded, and when Hiraga was sent overseas, his successor was convinced to add 12 fixed mounts.

Myoko class construction

Ship	Built at	Laid down	Launched	Commissioned
Myoko	Yokosuka Navy Yard	10/25/1924	04/16/1927	07/31/1929
Nachi	Kure Navy Yard	11/26/1924	06/15/1927	11/26/1928
Ashigara	Kobe by Kawasaki	04/11/1925	04/22/1928	08/20/1929
Haguro	Nagasaki by Mitsubishi	03/16/1925	03/24/1928	04/25/1929

In appearance, the ships resembled the previous class of cruisers. The *Myokos* presented a balanced, powerful appearance, with their profile dominated by a large bridge structure. As with the preceding classes, the *Myokos* ran into immediate problems with being over their design weight. Despite measures used to reduce the weight of the hull, the designed 2/3 trial displacement (11,850 tons) had reached 13,338 tons. This increase was partly due to the modifications made by the Naval General Staff, but the source of the majority of it remains unknown, according to Japanese sources. Given the fact that this unforeseen extra weight had adversely affected speed, radius, freeboard (thus submerging some of the armor belt), and reserve buoyancy, it is likely that the extra weight was not intentional.

Protection was improved over the previous classes, with armor and protective plates accounting for 16.1 percent of trial displacement. The main belt was 102mm and extended just over 404ft, enough to cover the machinery

Ashigara pictured from a US Navy ship off the coast of China in 1938. Only minor additional modifications were made before the start of the war. (Naval History and Heritage Command)

spaces, turret barbettes, and magazines. Deck armor included 32–35mm of steel armor on the middle deck and an upper deck composed of two layers, one with 16mm and the other of between 13 and 25mm. Turret barbettes were protected with a maximum of 76mm of armor.

Protection against underwater threats was provided by a system of longitudinal bulkheads and submerged bulkheads. The longitudinal bulkheads consisted of two 29mm plates that covered the side of the ship from the bottom of the main belt to the ship's double hull. The outer bulge ran 305ft and extended to a maximum depth of 8ft 2in. Altogether, the Japanese calculated that this system would be effective against a contact explosion of some 440lb of high-explosive.

Propulsion was provided by four propellers, each driven by a *Kampon* turbine. To achieve the design speed of 35.5 knots, 130,000shp was required. Twelve boilers were fitted and placed in nine boiler rooms. When the ships in the class conducted full-power trials, each posted speeds of more than 35 knots. Though the ships each carried 2,470 tons of oil, endurance was reduced from the designed 8,000nm to some 7,000nm due to the weight increase. This radius compared unfavorably with contemporary American and British cruisers.

Armament

The *Myoko* class was designed with five dual turrets of 7.9in guns, as intelligence indicated that contemporary Allied cruisers carried only eight main guns. Anti-aircraft protection was originally provided by six 4.7in high-angle guns in single mounts. A heavy torpedo armament featured six fixed 24in torpedo launchers on each beam.

Service modifications

Before the war, the class underwent major modernization. The first change occurred between 1931 and 1934, when the original 7.9in guns were replaced by 8in guns. In 1931, the Naval General Staff decided to upgrade the *Myoko* class further. This was carried out in a series of steps between 1934 and 1936. The first step was implemented in November 1934–June 1935 and was the most extensive. The fixed torpedo tube mounts were removed and replaced by two rotating quadruple mounts. The anti-aircraft protection was increased by the removal of the single 4.7in mounts in favor of four twin 5in high-angle guns. Above the new torpedo room, two catapults were fitted with adequate space for three aircraft. Protection was enhanced by the extension of the torpedo bulge. The various additions increased displacement by 680 tons, which reduced the top speed to 34 knots. In the second step, the placement and types of searchlights were improved and a pair of quadruple 13mm Hotchkiss machine-guns added. In the third step, the hull was reinforced and modifications made to the tripod mainmast and the foremast.

Plans for a second modernization were completed in June 1938, and executed in 1939. Modifications focused on upgrading the fire control and light anti-aircraft armament. Two additional quadruple torpedo mounts were fitted for a total of 16 tubes with 18 torpedo reloads. A heavier catapult was fitted, which allowed the ships to embark the newest type of reconnaissance seaplane. Despite the fact that the

Haguro seen from another *Myoko* class cruiser in 1937. In the foreground is a Type 89 dual-purpose twin mount and its Type 91 fire-control director. (Naval History and Heritage Command)

Myoko in May 1934. She has yet to undergo extensive modernization, but her original 7.9in main battery has been replaced with 8in guns. Note the single 4.7in high-angle guns still embarked and the original configuration of the aircraft-handling facilities. (Naval History and Heritage Command)

boilers were retubed, operational radius was decreased with the reduction of fuel capacity to 2,214 tons. This equated to an effective radius of 7,463nm at 14 knots. Crew size was increased to 891 (829 men and 62 officers). The weight increase of this modernization totaled 400 tons. As the anti-torpedo bulge was replaced with a larger one, this created a larger beam and thus a smaller draft. The larger beam also increased stability.

Wartime improvements centered around the addition of radar and the provision of a larger anti-aircraft guns. Between April and July 1943, all four ships returned to Japan for refit and modification. All received a No. 21 air-search radar mounted on top of the foremast and four additional twin 25mm mounts. A second round of modifications was made to the class, beginning in November 1943. Through March 1944, all four ships were fitted with eight single 25mm gun, and Nachi and Ashigara were fitted with No. 22 radars.

The third and final round of modernization was made after the battle of the Philippine Sea, when all four ships returned to Kure between June and September 1944. Myoko and Haguro received No. 22 radars and another four triple and 16 single 25mm guns. Nachi and Ashigara received two twin and 20 single 25mm mounts. All units also received a No. 13 radar. To save weight, the forward pair of searchlights was removed as well as the aft quadruple torpedo mounts. Only 16 torpedoes were carried – eight in the tubes with eight reloads.

Myoko class anti-aircraft fit, October 1944				
Ship	Triple mounts	Twin mounts	Single mounts	Total 25mm guns
Myoko	4	8	24	52
Haguro	4	8	24	52
Nachi	0	10	28	48
Ashigara	0	10	28	48

Wartime service

At the start of the war, the Myoko class comprised Sentai 4. All except Ashigara were assigned to cover the invasion of the southern Philippines at

THE *MYOKO* CLASS

The top profile and overhead view show the February 1942 configuration of Nachi as she appeared during the battle of the Java Sea. At this time, all four ships in the class were basically identical. The overall appearance of the Myokos was based on the IJN's previous scout cruiser classes, but with an expanded bridge structure and an increased armament. The quadruple torpedo launchers can be seen under the aircraft deck. The light anti-aircraft armament is clustered amidships in the form of four 25mm twin mounts.

By 1944, the appearance of the class had changed, as the bottom profile of Myoko in her October 1944 configuration indicates. Apart from minor variations in the placement of 25mm guns, all four ships in the class looked like this. Note the No. 21 radar on the foremast and the No. 13 radar on the mainmast. One of the quad torpedo mounts has been deleted, but a profusion of single and triple 25mm mounts have been added throughout the ship wherever a clear arc of fire can be gained.

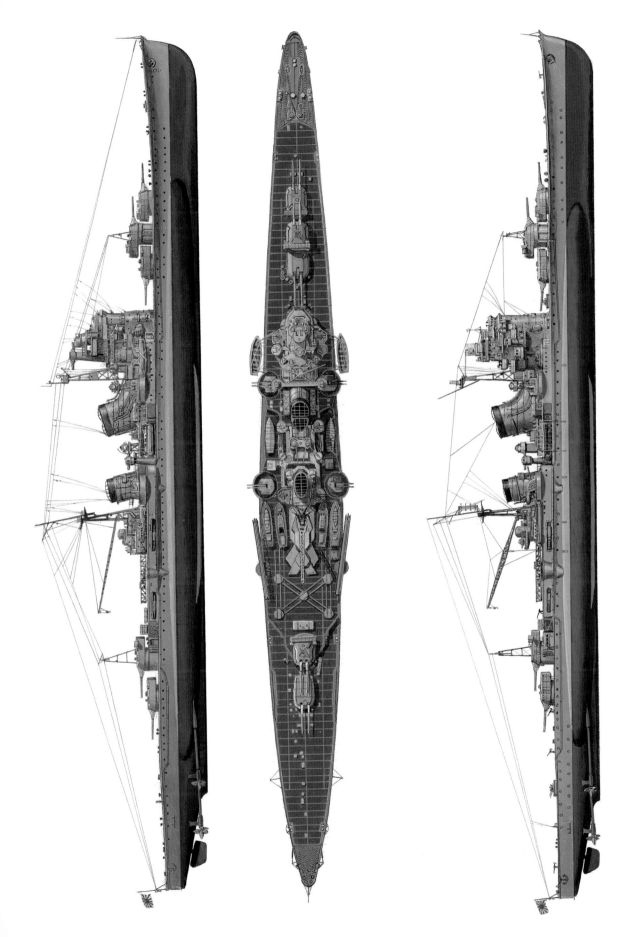

the start of war. On January 4, 1942, *Myoko* became the first Japanese heavy cruiser damaged during the war when she was hit by a single bomb from a B-17 while anchored in Davao Gulf; 35 men were killed and repairs took until February 20.

On February 27, 1942, *Nachi* and *Haguro* led a Japanese force against a mixed Dutch–British–American–Australian force. This engagement, known as the battle of the Java Sea, was the IJN's first opportunity to employ its favored tactic of massed torpedo attack. The results were a mixed bag. A torpedo from *Haguro* sank a Dutch destroyer, and early on February 28, torpedoes from *Haguro* and *Nachi* sank the Dutch cruisers *De Ruyter* and *Java*. These few hits decided the battle and opened Java to Japanese invasion. Yet the performance of the heavy cruisers was not up to Japanese expectations. During the height of the battle, 1,271 8in shells were fired from just under 22,000 yards to more than 27,000 yards; only five hit, and four of these were duds. Torpedo accuracy was also dismal, with *Haguro* firing 20 and *Nachi* 16; a total of 153 torpedoes were fired, with only three hits.

The victory at Java Sea was followed on March 1, 1942, with all four *Myokos* participating in the sinking by gunfire of the British heavy cruiser *Exeter* and a destroyer. Again, the quality of gunnery was an issue, with the four ships expending 1,459 rounds and 24 torpedoes. While *Ashigara* remained in the East Indies, *Myoko* and *Haguro* were then assigned as escorts to the main Japanese carrier force during the battle of Coral Sea in May 1942. They quickly returned north to participate in the battle of Midway in June. *Nachi* acted as flagship of the force dedicated to the invasion of the Aleutians.

Despite their formidable night combat capabilities, the *Myoko* class was not heavily involved in the struggle for Guadalcanal. *Myoko* bombarded Henderson Field during the night of October 15/16. Meanwhile, *Nachi* was assigned as the flagship of the Fifth Fleet responsible for operations in the North Pacific and *Ashigara* was active in the East Indies as flagship of the Second South Expeditionary Fleet.

In March 1943, *Nachi*, alongside the *Takao* class cruiser *Maya*, took part in the battle of Komandorski Islands while attempting to move troops and supplies to Japanese-occupied Attu Island in the Aleutians. *Nachi* launched torpedoes at enemy vessels with no result and a four-hour gun battle was inconclusive. The only American heavy cruiser present, *Salt Lake City*, was damaged, but no American ships were lost and the Japanese operation to supply the island was turned back. *Nachi* was damaged by five 5in shells with the loss of 14 men. Again, Japanese long-range cruiser gunnery had proved ineffective.

In late 1943, *Myoko* and *Haguro* were sent to Rabaul. The two cruisers formed the centerpiece of a Japanese surface action group that departed Rabaul on November 1, 1943, in response to the American invasion of Bougainville. The Japanese were unable to cope effectively with American radar-controlled gunnery and the night attack failed. *Myoko* was damaged in a collision with an escorting destroyer and *Haguro* received minor damage from some ten 5in and 6in shells, most of which were duds.

Nachi, later joined by *Ashigara* in April 1944, remained as the nucleus of the Fifth Fleet. Later, in June, *Myoko* and *Haguro* participated in

Myoko in March 1941 after completion of her second modernization. A second set of quadruple torpedo launchers was added in the forward part of the torpedo room, which can be seen in the opening under the forward part of the catapult. *Myoko* possessed a different bridge structure from her sisters with a separate tower for the director and the 8in gun rangefinder. (Yamato Museum)

the battle of the Philippine Sea, the largest carrier action of the war. Neither was damaged, but the battle resulted in the final destruction of the IJN's carrier arm.

When the Americans launched an attack on the Philippines in October 1944, the last resort of the IJN was to employ all its remaining heavy surface units to attack the American beachhead on Leyte Island. All four *Myoko* class were active in the resulting series of actions, known collectively as the battle of Leyte Gulf. *Myoko* and *Haguro* were assigned to the principal Japanese force, the First Diversionary Attack Force (also known as the Center Force). In a series of air attacks from American carriers on October 24 in the Sibuyan Sea, *Myoko* was struck by a single Mark 13 torpedo by aircraft from the carrier *Intrepid*. The torpedo struck the starboard side aft and put the starboard screws out of action. Since the ship could now only manage 15 knots, she was ordered to Singapore. After temporary repairs, *Myoko* was ordered to return to Japan. While en route, she was torpedoed again by the submarine *Bergall*; fires ignited and part of the stern broke off. After much effort, *Myoko* was towed back to Singapore, but assessed to be beyond repair. She was later moved to Seletar as a floating anti-aircraft battery. *Myoko* was surrendered in September 1945 at Seletar, one of only two cruisers to survive the war afloat. The ship was scuttled by the British in July 1946.

Nachi and *Ashigara* were also engaged at Leyte Gulf as part of the Second Diversionary Attack Force and ordered to enter Leyte Gulf from the south through Surigao Strait. In the later part of the battle of Surigao Strait, both cruisers launched eight torpedoes by radar against American units blocking the exit from the strait, then departed the battle area. During the retirement, *Nachi* collided with *Mogami*. *Nachi* proceeded to Manila, where American carrier aircraft sank the cruiser on November 5 off Cavite Naval Base. The cruiser was initially hit by about five bombs and two to three torpedoes and brought to a halt. Another wave of attacks literally tore the cruiser apart, with five torpedoes and 20 bomb strikes breaking her into three pieces. Only 220 crewmen survived the attack.

Ashigara participated in a December 26, 1944, attack on the American beachhead at San José on Mindoro Island in the Philippines. The vessel was hit by a 500lb bomb, but managed to bombard the American beachhead with more than 200 8in shells. In February 1945, *Ashigara* and *Haguro* were transferred to the Tenth Area

A fine overhead view of *Nachi* in 1941, showing her early war configuration. The large bridge remained after the ship's modernization, but unlike *Myoko*, a single tower on top of the bridge mounts both the fire-control director for the main battery and the rangefinder. Amidships are the four twin Type 89 5in guns and the four twin 25mm twin mounts located near the two smokestacks. Fire-control directors for the anti-aircraft weapons are also visible, as are four large searchlights for night combat grouped around the forward smokestack. The aircraft handling area was sufficient to embark three aircraft. (Yamato Museum)

Haguro in Simpson Harbor, Rabaul, on the morning of November 2, 1943. *Haguro* and *Myoko* had both just returned to Rabaul after the battle of Empress Augusta Bay. The battle was a debacle for the Japanese, with *Haguro* receiving minor damage, a light cruiser and destroyer sunk by American gunfire, and four Japanese ships damaged in collisions. Note the No. 21 radar on *Haguro's* foremast. (Naval History and Heritage Command)

Two *Myoko* class cruisers were assigned to the First Diversionary Attack Force during the battle of Leyte Gulf. This force was attacked by waves of American carrier aircraft in the Sibuyan Sea on October 24, 1944. This is one of the two *Myoko* class cruisers maneuvering under attack. Of note is the great amount of smoke produced by the 25mm guns, one of the many problems with the standard Japanese light anti-aircraft gun. *Haguro* was undamaged in these attacks, but *Myoko* was struck by an aircraft-launched torpedo that forced her to retire. (Naval History and Heritage Command)

Fleet and were tasked with transporting troops and supplies around the Dutch East Indies and to islands in the Bay of Bengal. While transiting from Batavia to Singapore on June 8, 1945, *Ashigara* was attacked by the Royal Navy submarine HMS *Trenchant*. The submarine delivered a well-planned attack and hit the cruiser with five torpedoes. The ship sank with heavy loss of life among the 1,600 army troops onboard.

Haguro's luck ran out in May 1945 during an operation to run supplies to the Andaman Islands. Early on May 16, four Royal Navy destroyers executed a brilliant assault, launching 37 torpedoes at short-range. At least three hit the cruiser, which sank with heavy loss of life. This was the last major surface action of World War II.

Myoko class specifications (after second reconstruction)	
Displacement:	15,933 tons (full load)
Dimensions:	Length 668ft 6in overall; beam 68ft; draft 36ft
Speed:	33 knots
Range:	7,463nm at 14 knots
Crew:	920 in *Haguro* and *Nachi* (*sentai* flagships); 970 in *Myoko* and *Ashigara* (fitted as fleet flagships)

Takao Class
Design and construction

The *Takao* class was an improved version of the *Myoko* class. The chief designer was Constructor Captain Fujimoto, who had succeeded Rear Admiral Hiraga. For the hull, powerplant, protection, and main gun configuration, Fujimoto decided to go with that already used for the *Myoko* class. The differences would be in a new type of 8in gun that possessed a greater elevation and was therefore thought to be suitable for anti-aircraft work, and in the substitution of rotating torpedo mounts, which were placed on the main deck. Protection was increased and an additional catapult fitted. Aesthetically, the two classes looked dramatically different, as the new class was planned to fit a massive bridge structure.

Since the design of the class pre-dated the trials of the preceding *Myoko* class, the same issues of excessive weight existed. Despite weight-saving measures, the displacement was 10 percent greater than designed. The total weight of the class devoted to armor and protective plates was 2,368 tons or 16.8 percent of total displacement. This was some 340 tons greater than in the

Takao class construction				
Ship	Built at	Laid down	Launched	Commissioned
Takao	Yokosuka Navy Yard	04/28/1927	05/12/1930	05/31/1932
Atago	Kure Navy Yard	04/28/1927	06/16/1930	03/30/1932
Maya	Kobe by Kawasaki	12/04/1928	11/08/1930	06/30/1932
Chokai	Nagasaki by Mitsubishi	03/26/1928	04/05/1931	06/30/1932

Myoko class. Protection was on the same scale as the *Myoko* class, but with slight modifications. The area included in the fore and aft armored bulkheads was shorter, as was the side armor belt. However, protection over the fore and aft magazines was heavier. Underwater protection was comparable to the *Myoko* class, with the anti-torpedo bulkheads being calculated to be able to withstand a 440lb high-explosive charge.

The salient design feature was the massive new bridge, with three times the volume of *Myoko*'s bridge. Though the weight of such a large structure added to an already overweight design, designers decided the price was worth paying to provide a central location for the increasingly complex equipment needed to conduct gunnery and torpedo combat at greater ranges. Fire control for the main battery and the 4.7in anti-aircraft guns, as well as for the torpedo battery, was located in the bridge structure. Also included were spaces for navigation, communication and for command and staff personnel. Some of the vital areas were provided with 10mm steel plates for protection against aircraft machine guns.

The aircraft facilities on the *Takao* class were improved over the previous classes. Two catapults were fitted and enough room was provided for three aircraft. The propulsion system was similar to that on *Myoko*. Four shafts developed a total of 130,000shp. All four ships developed speeds of 35 knots or greater during trials. The design endurance was 8,000nm at 14 knots, but the excess weight meant that this range was reduced by some 1,000nm.

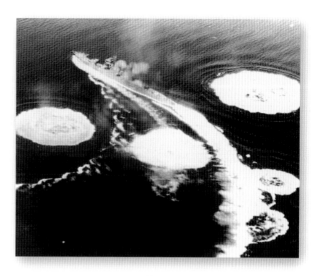

Nachi under attack from carrier aircraft from US Navy Task Group 38.3 in Manila Bay on November 5, 1944. The ship was photographed by aircraft from the US carrier *Essex*. At this point in the attack, she remains undamaged. (Naval History and Heritage Command)

Armament

The armament for the *Takao* class was identical in layout to that of the *Myoko* class. The only real difference was the mounting of a new type of 8in gun, which was designed for both anti-surface and anti-aircraft fire. To accomplish its intended anti-aircraft duties, the gun turrets were designed to have a maximum elevation of 70 degrees. In practice, though, it was found that only a 55-degree elevation was possible. Protection of the turrets was provided by 25mm of armor all round, sufficient only to give the gun crew splinter protection. The promise of the new 8in gun as an anti-aircraft weapon, however, was never realized. The designed firing rate was 5rpm, but since the gun had to be brought down to 5 degrees to load (taking eight seconds to depress and elevate), this was never attained. The training speed of such a large turret was also inadequate for anti-aircraft work.

The failure of the 8in gun as an anti-aircraft weapon meant the burden of air defense fell to single 4.7in guns. The *Takao* class fitted only four of these weapons, unlike the six on the *Myoko* class. Close-in air defense was provided by two 40mm Vickers guns and two 7.7mm Vickers machine-guns. Both were found to be ineffective and were replaced by 13mm and 25mm Japanese-designed weapons in 1935.

The fourth wave of attacking US aircraft, including torpedo bombers from the carrier *Lexington*, delivered a devastating attack on the immobile cruiser. As many as five torpedoes hit the ship, blowing off the bow and the stern following the explosion of the aft magazine. The result of the attack is shown in this photo. Only 220 men survived the sinking and subsequent strafing by American aircraft; 807 were killed, including 74 from the embarked Fifth Fleet staff. (Naval History and Heritage Command)

Atago in her original configuration, before her major 1938–39 modernization. During this modernization, the size of her enormous bridge superstructure was reduced and her masts shortened. (Naval History and Heritage Command)

As built, the *Takao* class featured rotating torpedo mounts in place of the fixed mounts on earlier classes. Measures were taken to reduce the damage to the ship if the torpedoes were hit during combat. The mounts were located outside of the hull and mounted on sponsons to extend beyond the hull surface. In action, the tubes could be trained further away from the ship's hull, and the warheads were protected by a steel casing when not in the tubes. Originally, 12 tubes were planned, but this number was reduced to eight due to weight and space issues. In addition to the eight torpedoes located in the tubes, another 16 were carried as reloads. By means of a system of aerial rails in the torpedo rooms, a second broadside could be fired within three minutes of the first and a third eight minutes later.

Service modifications

Plans for modernizing the *Takao* class were complete by April 1938, but the approach of war meant that only two ships in the class were fully modernized: *Takao* at Yokosuka from May 1938 to August 1939 and *Atago* from April 1938 to October 1939. *Chokai* and *Maya* received only limited modernization before the war, including modifications to handle the Type 93 oxygen-propelled torpedo, heavier catapults, and the standard fit of 13mm and 25mm light anti-aircraft guns.

During the modernization, the anti-aircraft armament was increased, though the projected fit of the Type 89 5in twin guns did not begin until after the start of the war: *Atago* and *Takao* received theirs in May 1942; *Chokai* retained the single 4.7in guns until she was lost in 1944; *Maya* kept hers until reconstruction as an anti-aircraft cruiser began in November 1943. The light anti-aircraft armament was standardized and in the autumn of 1941 the two twin 13mm mounts were replaced with two 25mm mounts. The torpedo armament was augmented by the substitution of quad mounts for the existing double torpedo mounts.

The largest change was to the bridge structure, which was rebuilt to reduce topweight. When completed, the bridge was much smaller in appearance and was the primary feature for distinguishing *Atago* and *Takao* from their sisters *Maya* and *Chokai*. The bridge accommodated new fire-control equipment and featured the placement of an almost 20ft rangefinder in a separate tower immediately aft of the Type 94 fire-control director.

The other primary change was the alteration of the aircraft-handling facilities and the area of the hangar. To do this, the mainmast was moved 82ft aft. Two heavier catapults were also fitted and moved forward. As on the *Myoko* class, larger bulges were fitted to increase anti-torpedo protection and stability.

Chokai pictured off the Chinese coast in 1938. The massive bridge structure is clearly evident and was retained by Chokai until sunk in 1944. The Chokai was the least modified of her class during the war. (Naval History and Heritage Command)

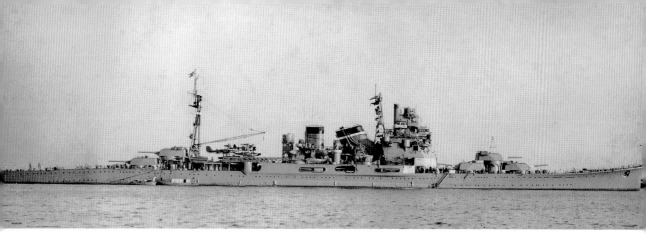

During the war, modifications were made to the ships' radar and light anti-aircraft fit. In July–August 1943, *Atago* and *Takao* received the foremast-mounted No. 21 radar and two triple 25mm guns, making their total light anti-aircraft fit six twin and two triple mounts. *Maya* and *Chokai* received the No. 21 radar and two twin 25mm mounts between August and September, making their total anti-aircraft fit eight twin mounts.

In November 1943–January 1944, *Atago* and *Takao* were fitted with No. 22 radars and eight 25mm single guns. *Chokai* could not return to Japan during this period, but was given ten single 25mm guns at Truk. After receiving severe damage in November 1943, *Maya* returned to Yokosuka in December 1943 for repair and conversion into an anti-aircraft cruiser. Her No. 3 8in gun turret was removed, as were all her twin 25mm mounts, the single 4.7in mounts, and her old twin torpedo tubes. In their place were fitted six twin Type 89 guns with two Type 94 directors, plus 13 triple and nine single Type 96 guns. In addition, 36 13mm machine-guns on moveable mounts and four quadruple torpedo mounts with no reserve torpedoes were fitted. A No. 22 radar was added, and the No. 21 radar received a larger antenna.

Another round of modernization began after the battle of the Philippine Sea in June 1944. All four units received a No. 13 radar and *Chokai* finally received a No. 22 set. In June 1944, *Atago* and *Takao* received four triple and 22 single 25mm guns. *Maya* received another 18 single guns, while *Chokai* received 12 more single mounts. Plans were made to convert her as *Maya*, but since she did not return to Japan until June 1944, these was never carried out.

Wartime service

The four units of the *Takao* class comprised *Sentai 4* at the start of the war. All were initially deployed into the South China Sea to support the Japanese invasion of Malaya. In January and February 1942, *Sentai 4* provided distant cover for the invasion of the Dutch East Indies. In late February, the unit moved south of Java to catch fleeing Allied ships – eight were sunk, including the American destroyer *Pillsbury*.

A fine beam view of *Takao* in December 1939 after modernization. The principal changes during modernization were the reduction in the size of the bridge and the movement of the mainmast further aft. The new bridge structure was topped with the main battery director and a rangefinder measuring almost 20ft. Unlike in the *Myoko* class, the *Takao* class placed their torpedo launchers forward, as shown here, and not aft under the aircraft deck. The three aircraft embarked in this view include one Type 94 Alf and two Type 95 reconnaissance seaplanes (Allied codename "Dave"). (Yamato Museum)

Takao class anti-aircraft fit, October 1944				
Ship	Triple mounts	Twin mounts	Single mounts	Total 25mm guns
Takao	6	6	30	60
Atago	6	6	30	60
Maya	13	0	27	66
Chokai	0	8	22	38

C HIJMS *TAKAO*

This view depicts *Takao* as she appeared in October 1944 before the Battle of Leyte Gulf. *Takao* was the lead ship of the Imperial Navy's most powerful class of heavy cruisers. After an eventful wartime career, *Takao* was heavily damaged at Leyte Gulf by submarine torpedoes and sat out the remainder of the war in Singapore. *Takao* is shown with all wartime modifications, principally an augmented anti-aircraft suite and the addition of radar.

Key

1. 20.3cm/50-cal Model E Gun Turret (5)
2. Type 89 12.7cm/40-cal High Angle Gun (2 shown)
3. Type 96 25mm Triple Machine Gun (4 shown)
4. Type 96 25mm Double Machine Gun (3 shown)
5. Type 96 25mm Single Machine Gun (10 shown)
6. Type 92 Quadruple Torpedo Mount (2 shown)
7. Type 92 110cm Searchlight (2 shown)
8. 60cm Signaling Searchlight
9. Type 94 Low Angle Director Tower
10. 6m Rangefinder
11. Anti-aircraft Platform
12. Navigation Bridge
13. 4.5m High Angle Rangefinder
14. Type 91 High Angle Director (for 12.7cm guns)
15. Auxiliary Main Gun Director
16. No. 21 Radar
17. No. 13 Radar
18. No. Radar
19. Kure Number 2, Model 5 Catapult
20. Type 0 Long Range Reconnaissance Floatplane
21. Number 3 Boiler Room
22. Number 4 Boiler Room
23. Number 6 Boiler Room
24. Number 8 Boiler Room
25. Low Pressure Turbine
26. Cruising Turbine
27. Condensers
28. Generator Room
29. Type 95 Machine Gun Control Tower
30. Foremast
31. Radar Room
32. Forward Smokestack
33. Aft Smokestack
34. Mainmast
35. 20m Aircraft Crane

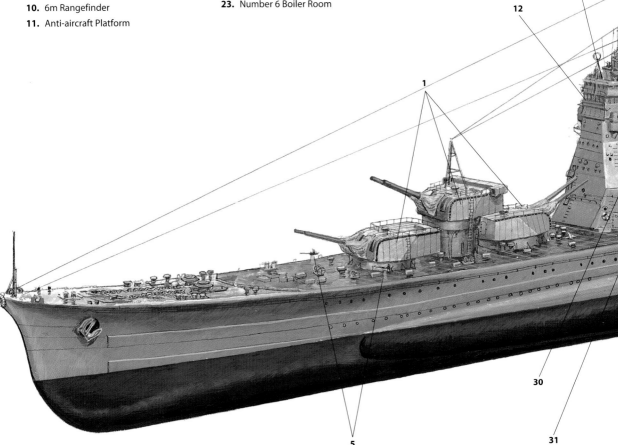

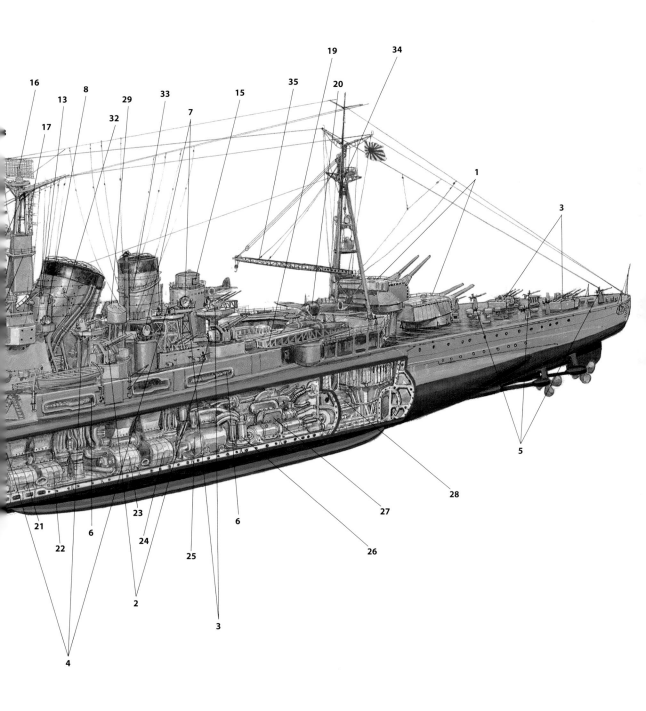

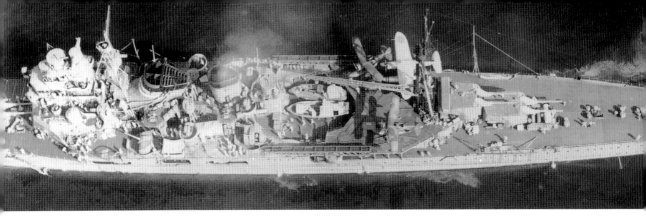

A fine overhead view of *Atago* in 1941. As on *Takao*, the bridge has been extensively reworked. The ship still retains her single 4.7in high-angle guns, as these were not replaced with the Type 89 twin 5in guns until 1942. The embarked aircraft include two camouflaged Type 95s and a standard light-gray painted Type 0. (Yamato Museum)

Chokai was assigned to take part in the April 1942 Indian Ocean raid as the flagship of Vice Admiral Ozawa Jisaburo's Mobile Force. In June 1942, both *Atago* and *Chokai* were assigned to the abortive Midway operation, while *Takao* and *Maya* took part in the Japanese seizure of two Aleutian islands.

Continuing in her role as a fleet flagship, *Chokai* was assigned to the Eighth Fleet in August 1942. As the flagship of Vice Admiral Mikawa Gunichi, she played a central role in the Japanese victory at Savo Island, although she also received the most damage of any Japanese ship present – American cruisers achieved several hits, killing 34 crewmen. Throughout the campaign, *Chokai* was a regular visitor to the waters around Guadalcanal, and on 14 October she and *Kinugasa* bombarded Henderson Field. On November 3, the other three ships of *Sentai 4* departed Truk to reinforce the Eighth Fleet. Later, on November 13, *Maya* and *Chokai* left Shortland anchorage to conduct a night bombardment of Henderson Field alongside *Suzuya*. After hitting the airfield with 989 shells, the cruisers were attacked during their withdrawal by aircraft from the carrier *Enterprise*. *Kinugasa* was sunk, *Chokai* slightly damaged, and *Maya* more heavily damaged when a dive-bomber struck the ship's mainmast and crashed into her port side, igniting fires. *Maya's* torpedoes were jettisoned to avoid a disaster and she was sent back to Japan for repairs.

The second naval battle of Guadalcanal, during the night of November 14/15, pitted a Japanese task force centered around the fast battleship *Kirishima*, plus *Atago* and *Takao*, against a smaller American task force with the battleships *South Dakota* and *Washington*. The scenario seemed a favorable one for the IJN, with a large force of destroyers led by two of its finest heavy cruisers working at night against an improvised American force operating in confined waters. *Atago* and *Takao* each launched eight torpedoes at *Washington* from a mere 4,000 yards' range, but all missed. The cruisers did succeed in scoring at least 16 8in hits on *South Dakota*, but caused no critical damage to the heavily armored battleship. At the conclusion of the battle, the Americans emerged victorious when *Kirishima* was sunk by *Washington* and the Japanese plan to bombard Henderson Field was thwarted.

After her repairs, *Maya* was assigned to the Fifth Fleet and took part with *Nachi* in the March 1943 battle of Komandorski Islands, as already recounted. Later that year, *Takao*, *Atago*, *Maya*, and other heavy cruisers were forward-deployed to Rabaul with the aim of launching a massive cruiser attack on the American invasion forces at Empress Augusta Bay on Bougainville. To forestall such an operation, the Americans hastily mounted a carrier air attack on the cruisers on November 5, while the Japanese vessels were still anchored in Rabaul Harbor. *Takao* was hit by a bomb near No. 2 turret, killing 23 men; she departed the same day with *Atago* for Truk. *Atago*

suffered three near misses that caused flooding in the boiler and engine rooms. *Maya* was heavily damaged when a dive-bomber hit the aircraft deck above the No. 3 engine room and started a major fire in the engine room itself that killed 70. *Maya* returned to Japan in December 1943 and underwent major repairs and conversion.

The entire *Takao* class participated in the Philippine Sea operation. *Maya* was slightly damaged by near misses from carrier air attack. Leyte Gulf, however, was the death knell of the IJN's finest class of cruisers. All four were assigned to the First Diversionary Attack Force. On October 23, the force was ambushed by two American submarines in the Palawan Passage. *Darter* sank *Atago* with four torpedoes and hit *Takao* with two others, setting her afire and stopping her dead in the water. *Dace* sank *Maya* with four torpedoes, killing 470 of 1,105 crewmen. *Takao* was able to get under way and arrived in Singapore on November 12. The cruiser was deemed irreparable and was moved to join *Myoko* in Seletar Harbor as a floating anti-aircraft battery.

Only *Chokai* remained to take part in the October 25, 1944, battle off Samar against American escort carriers and destroyers. *Chokai* was engaged by the destroyer escort *Samuel B. Roberts* with her 5in guns. Minutes after being hit amidships, a secondary explosion, caused by her own torpedoes, knocked out *Chokai*'s propulsion system and rudder. She was then attacked by aircraft from the escort carrier *Kitkun Bay* and hit by 500lb bombs and brought to a stop. Later that morning, the crew was taken off by a destroyer and the cruiser scuttled. All survivors were killed when the destroyer was sunk two days later by American carrier aircraft.

During the night of July 30/31, 1945, the Royal Navy attacked the two surviving damaged heavy cruisers in Seletar Harbor. *Myoko* was undamaged, but the midget submarine *XE3* successfully approached *Takao* and placed six limpet mines under the ship's keel. The blasts of some of the mines blew a 23x10ft hole in the ship's hull and created other serious damage, but she miraculously stayed afloat. She was surrendered in September 1945 and scuttled in October 1946.

Chokai at Truk in October 1942. Behind her is superbattleship *Yamato*. Because of her flagship duties, she was not heavily modified during the war, as is evident in this shot – she retains her single 4.7in guns and twin torpedo mounts. The aircraft is a Type 94 "Alf" floatplane. (Yamato Museum)

This is the only close-up photo of *Maya* as an anti-aircraft cruiser. The view is from May 1944 and was almost certainly taken at Lingga Roads, where the First Mobile Force was stationed in preparation for a decisive battle. This view clearly shows how the 8in No. 3 turret was replaced by a pair of twin 5in guns and three triple 25mm guns. (Yamato Museum)

Takao class specifications (Takao and Atago after reconstruction)	
Displacement:	15,186 tons (full load) (Takao and Atago 15,641 tons)
Dimensions:	Length 668ft 6in overall; beam 67ft (Takao and Atago 68ft); draft 36ft
Speed:	35.5 knots
Range:	7,000nm at 14 knots
Crew:	900–920 by 1941, and if a fleet staff was embarked, this increased further to 970. Wartime modifications brought the crew to approximately 1,100

Mogami Class

Design and construction

Design of the first class of Japanese light cruiser to be built fully under Washington Treaty restrictions began in 1930. The Naval General Staff gave the design team the same basic requirements used for the 10,000-ton class cruisers, with the salient exception that these 8,500-ton ships were armed with 15 6.1in guns instead of the usual 8in battery. However, the design had to accommodate the upgrade from 6.1in to 8in as soon as the treaty ceased to apply. Torpedo armament remained heavy – 12 tubes in triple mounts. Design speed was set at 37 knots. As in the earlier heavy cruiser designs, the magazines required protection against 8in shells and the machinery spaces were protected against 6in shells. This set of design requirements was literally impossible to achieve on such a small displacement, even with extensive electric welding to save weight. The design adopted in 1931 was overweight at 9,500 tons. The original *Mogami* design borrowed much from the *Takao* class. There were noticeable differences, however. The arrangement of the front three turrets was altered and the *Mogami* vessels used a single smokestack instead of two. The ship's heavy anti-aircraft armament was increased with the addition of 5in twin mounts.

Predictably, the original design ran into trouble. The launch of the first two ships in the class, *Mogami* and *Mikuma*, came just after the capsizing of the torpedo-boat *Tomozuru* on March 12, 1934. This disaster prompted a study on the stability of the IJN's ships, and when the report on the incident was completed in June, several major design changes were decided for the new class of overweight cruisers. To reduce weight and lower the center of gravity, the large bridge structure copied from the *Takao* design was replaced by a much smaller version. A smaller foremast was also substituted. The seaplane hangar was removed, as were the large structures around the mainmast. When the lead ship commenced trials in March 1935, many problems were also found with the electrically welded hull. After repairs, *Mogami* and *Mikuma* joined the

 TAKAO CLASS CRUISER CHOKAI

This scene depicts *Chokai* departing Rabaul Harbor on the afternoon of August 7, 1942, en route to attack the American invasion fleet off Guadalcanal. During the battle of Savo Island on August 9, *Chokai*, as the flagship of Vice Admiral Mikawa Gunichi, played a key role in the largest Japanese surface victory of the naval war in the Pacific. In the night engagement, *Chokai* was responsible for the majority of damage inflicted on the American heavy cruiser *Astoria*, which later sank. During the battle, *Chokai* expended 308 8in rounds, 120 4.7in rounds, and eight torpedoes. *Chokai* was the least modified of the *Takao* class cruisers throughout the war. In August 1942, she retained her large bridge structure and the single 4.7in high-angle guns she was commissioned with. By October 1944, when she was lost, the only difference in her appearance was the addition of radar and 25mm light anti-aircraft guns.

A fine port-quarter view of *Mogami* in August 1935. Despite her impressive and compact appearance, the ship was taken in for reconstruction in 1936 to address stability concerns. (Yamato Museum)

fleet for maneuvers in September 1935, and during a typhoon minor hull damage was incurred. Both units were placed out of service for the second time; trials on the next ship, *Suzuya*, were stopped, as was construction of the final ship in the class, *Kumano*.

The subsequent reconstruction included the replacement of the welded hull plates with riveted plates and an expanded bulge to enhance stability. These structural improvements added some 1,000 tons in weight, which meant that when *Mogami* was finally completed, she was 1,800 tons over her design displacement. Reconstruction delayed the recommissioning of *Mogami* until February 1938; *Mikuma* and *Suzuya* had their re-work completed by October 1937. *Kumano* was completed with the modifications being fitted to the rest of the class, and was commissioned the same day as *Suzuya*.

Mogami class construction				
Ship	**Built at**	**Laid down**	**Launched**	**Commissioned**
Mogami	Kure Navy Yard	10/27/1931	03/14/1934	07/28/1935
Mikuma	Nagasaki by Mitsubishi	12/24/1931	05/31/1934	08/29/1935
Suzuya	Yokosuka Navy Yard	12/11/1933	11/20/1934	10/31/1937
Kumano	Kobe by Kawasaki	04/05/1934	10/15/1936	10/31/1937

Suzuya in November 1935, running full-power trials. Note that the ship is not yet complete, as it is missing the main rangefinder, the aft 5in twin mounts, and all light anti-aircraft guns. Shortly after this photo was taken, on November 20, 1935, *Suzuya's* trials were suspended due to concerns over stability. (Yamato Museum)

Japan withdrew from the Washington Treaty on December 29, 1934, and on January 15, 1936, decided not to sign the Second London Naval Treaty. This meant that the *Mogami* class modernization could proceed without regard to weight or armament restrictions. The Japanese accordingly planned to replace the existing 6.1in guns with 8in guns, mount heavier catapults, and increase the torpedo armament. This work was completed between September 1939 and April 1940.

Protection for the *Mogami* class was similar to previous classes of heavy cruisers, with a main belt of a maximum 100mm of armor and enhanced protection over magazine spaces of up to 140mm. Overhead protection included an armored deck of 35mm and an additional 40mm on the lower deck over the magazines. The propulsion system was more efficient and powerful than that fitted on the *Myoko* and *Takao* classes. A total of 152,000shp was generated to meet the design requirement of 37 knots. Since the ships were overweight, however, the design speed was not reached, though all four ships attained 34–35 knots during full-power trials.

Armament

When completed, the *Mogami* class mounted 15 6.1in guns in five triple turrets. The No. 2 turret was mounted

directly behind No. 1 turret and could only fire broadside. Anti-aircraft armament was the standard eight 5in guns in four twin mounts, four twin 25mm mounts amidships, and a pair of 13mm machine guns forward of the bridge. The torpedo armament was 12 tubes in four triple mounts, mounted two per side. In 1939–40, ten 8in guns in five turrets replaced the 6.1in guns.

Kumano pictured off the Chinese coast in 1938 with her original triple 6.1in turrets. The ship was re-armed with 8in guns by 1940. (Naval History and Heritage Command)

Service modifications

Mikuma was lost at Midway before any wartime modifications were made. *Mogami* was badly damaged in the same battle and, as will be described below, she was selected for the most extensive modification of any IJN cruiser. For the remainder of the war, modifications focused on improving air defense capability. In fact, plans were made in late 1942/early 1943 for the conversion of *Suzuya* and *Kumano* into anti-aircraft cruisers by removing their 8in guns in favor of additional Type 89 5in mounts, but these were not carried out. These units received a No. 21 radar on top of the foremast and four triple 25mm gun mounts, two in front of the bridge in place of the 13mm machine guns and two by the mainmast. In March–April 1944, eight single 25mm guns were added. After the battle of Philippine Sea in June 1944, further modifications were made with the addition of two No. 22 radars on the foremast and a No. 13 radar mounted on the forward part of the mainmast. Four more triple 25mm mounts were also fitted, two near the bridge and two on the stern. *Suzuya* received ten single mounts and *Kumano* 16.

After being damaged at Midway, *Mogami* returned to Japan in August 1942. One of the Japanese lessons from the battle was that the numbers of scouting aircraft operating from the cruisers were inadequate. Accordingly, it was decided to convert *Mogami* into an aircraft cruiser. This entailed the removal of the two aft 8in turrets and the extension of the aircraft deck to the stern of the ship, providing room for 11 seaplanes. During the course of this reconstruction, a No. 21 radar was added on the foremast and the previous light anti-aircraft fit was removed and replaced by ten triple 25mm mounts. When *Mogami* was under repair after her November 1943 damage, eight additional single 25mm mounts were added on the aircraft deck. Ten more single mounts were added in June 1944, together with four 25mm triple mounts.

Wartime service

The four *Mogami* warships formed *Sentai* 7 at the start of the war. In the initial weeks of the conflict this unit covered invasion convoys destined for Malaya and British Borneo. Not until the landings on Java did the *Mogami* class vessels see their first action. In the aftermath of the battle of the Java Sea, *Mogami* and *Mikuma* engaged the American heavy cruiser *Houston* and the Australian light cruiser *Perth* in the battle of Sunda Strait on the night of February 28–March 1. The two Allied cruisers were sunk under a hail of torpedoes and searchlight-directed gunfire from the two Japanese cruisers and their escorting destroyers. Unfortunately for the Japanese, in the confusion *Mogami* sank five Japanese units (four army transports and a minesweeper) when her torpedoes missed the intended target (*Houston*)

Ship	Triple mounts	Twin mounts	Single mounts	Total 25mm guns
Mogami	14	0	18	60
Suzuya	8	4	18	50
Kumano	8	4	24	56

and ran into the anchorage of the invasion fleet. Investigations later in the war confirmed that *Mogami* was the culprit, not the destroyer *Fubuki* as first thought.

Following operations to cover landings in northern Sumatra, the cruisers joined *Chokai* for the Indian Ocean raid. Split into two groups, *Sentai 7* accounted for eight Allied merchant ships.

Next up for *Sentai 7* was the invasion of Midway. The cruisers made up the Close Support Group with responsibility for shelling the island prior to a Japanese landing. After the battle turned against the IJN, and in an attempt to retrieve the situation, *Sentai 7* was ordered to close the island on June 5 and destroy the airfield. When reason finally prevailed, the bombardment was cancelled, but by this time the cruisers were only 90 miles from the island. While executing the turn to the east to depart the area, a submarine was spotted and, in the subsequent maneuvers, *Mogami* accidentally rammed *Mikuma*. *Mikuma* was still able to steer, but *Mogami's* bow was heavily damaged and her speed reduced to 21 knots.

The two undamaged cruisers from *Sentai 7* were ordered to depart the area at high speed, but the ordeal of the two damaged ships now began in earnest. On the morning of June 7, American carrier dive-bombers launched three attacks on the two cruisers. The first placed two bombs on *Mogami*. The crew had taken the earlier precaution of jettisoning the torpedoes, so a fire in the area of the torpedo room was put out with no further damage. The second attack was devastating, with two more hits on *Mogami* and at least five on *Mikuma*. Fires in the engine room brought *Mikuma* to a halt, and when they spread to the torpedo room, her torpedoes exploded and demolished the aft part of the superstructure. The final wave of attackers deposited another bomb on *Mogami*; although she did not sink, her total casualties were 92 dead and 101 wounded. *Mikuma* finally sank on the evening of June 7 with the loss of precisely 700 of her crew. She was the first Japanese cruiser lost in the war.

THE *MOGAMI* CLASS

The top profile is of *Mikuma* during the Japanese conquest of the Dutch East Indies and depicts the ship in her early war configuration. The four ships of the *Mogami* class presented a different appearance than the previous classes of Japanese heavy cruisers, with their single smokestack and the altered arrangement of the three forward 8in turrets.

The second profile and overhead view is of *Mogami* in 1944 following her conversion into a hybrid cruiser-carrier. This was by far the most extensive wartime modernization of a Japanese cruiser. The two aft 8in turrets have been removed and the aircraft deck extended to the stern. This permitted as many as 11 floatplanes to be embarked. By this point in the war, the standard cruiser floatplane was the Navy Type 0 reconnaissance seaplane (E13A1), given the codename "Jake" by the Allies. In October 1944, *Mogami* became the only cruiser to embark the navy reconnaissance seaplane *Zuiun* ("Auspicious Cloud") Model 11 (Allied codename "Paul"), which was intended to replace the Type 0 seaplane. No hangar was provided for the embarked aircraft. Radars include the No. 21 on the foremast and the No. 13 on the mainmast. The light anti-aircraft gun fit consisted of a mix of triple and single 25mm mounts.

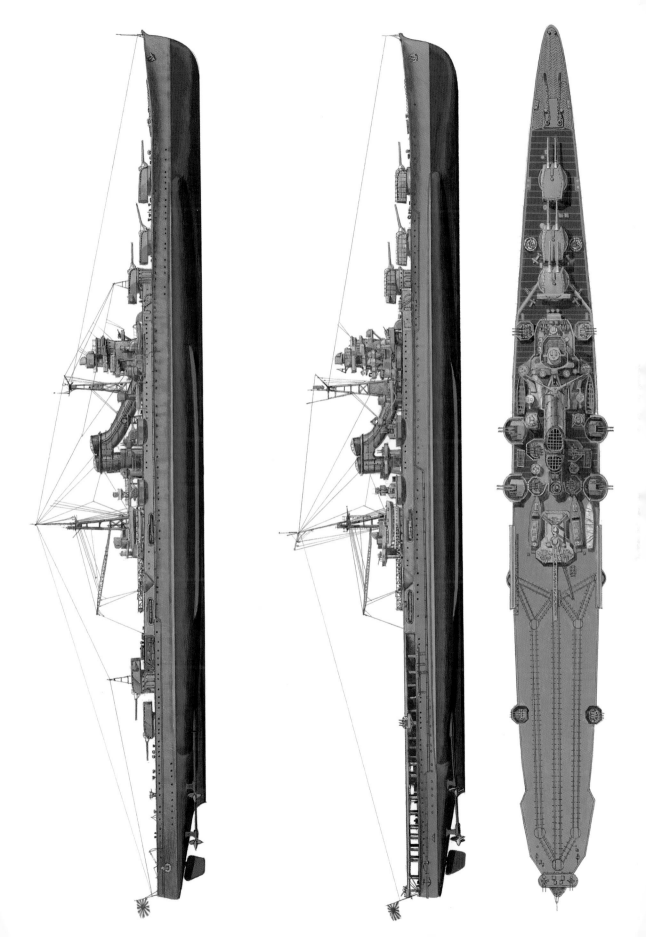

This March 1939 shot shows the forward three turrets on *Kumano*. Despite the greater rate of fire of the 6.1in triple turrets shown here (twice as much as an 8in turret), the Japanese preferred the slightly longer range and considerably greater penetrating power of the 8in guns. (Naval History and Heritage Command)

The remnants of *Sentai 7* were moved to the South Pacific after the American invasion of Guadalcanal. Both cruisers were active in the carrier battles of Eastern Solomons and Santa Cruz, and were undamaged. *Suzuya* was ordered to reinforce the Eighth Fleet in early November. On the night of November 13–14, *Suzuya* bombarded Henderson Field with 504 shells.

Sentai 7 remained active in the Solomons into 1943. On July 20, off the island of Kolombangara, aircraft from Guadalcanal attacked *Kumano* and scored a near miss that caused major flooding. *Kumano* was forced to return to Japan for repairs. *Mogami* was caught in Rabaul Harbor in November 1943 and subjected to the same carrier air attack that devastated units of the *Takao* class. Though she was hit by only a single 500lb bomb, the damage to the forward part of the ship was severe and she was also forced to return to Japan.

The battle of Leyte Gulf in 1944 marked the end of the *Mogami* class. All three remaining ships were committed; two were lost during the battle and the third damaged. *Mogami* was assigned to the 3rd Section of the First Diversionary Attack Force. After suffering minor damage due to carrier air attack in the Sulu Sea on October 24, *Mogami* and the rest of her task group tried to force the Surigao Strait the next night. *Mogami* came under heavy fire from American cruisers and was hit by four or five 8in shells, which killed the ship's commanding officer and started a fire amidships. Retreating south down the strait, *Mogami* then collided with *Nachi* and, as the fires spread, five of her torpedoes exploded, causing additional damage. Her ordeal was far from over, however, as she was hit by another 10–20 6 and 8in rounds from American cruisers. In spite of all this, it appeared as if *Mogami* would actually survive her fearful pounding, but when the remaining engine stopped, the ship went dead in the water. At this point, she was attacked by carrier aircraft and hit by two bombs forward. The acting captain ordered the ship abandoned when attempts to flood one of the forward magazines failed. *Mogami* was scuttled by a destroyer later in the day; 192 of the crew were killed.

Suzuya was also lost on October 25. While engaging American escort carriers off Samar, she suffered a near miss from a bomb that reduced her speed. A second near miss was more serious. This ignited the torpedoes in the forward starboard torpedo tubes, starting a large fire that was fed by the explosion of additional torpedoes. An hour later, the remaining torpedoes exploded as well as the 5in rounds for the Type 89 guns, and the entire ship was set ablaze.

A very clear shot of *Mogami's* starboard side in August 1943, taken at Truk. Two Type 89 twin 5in guns are evident, as are two triple Type 96 25mm guns behind them. On the flight deck are five Type 0 "Jake" reconnaissance aircraft. (Yamato Museum)

Kumano also came off poorly in the battle off Samar on October 25. Early in the fight she was hit by a single torpedo launched from destroyer *Johnston*. The torpedo struck the bow and reduced her speed to 12 knots. She was ordered to return to Singapore. Transiting the Sibuyan Sea the next day, she was attacked by carrier aircraft and suffered three 500lb bomb hits.

Kumano arrived in Manila on October 28 for temporary repairs; she departed November 4 to escort a convoy and return to Japan. On November 6, the cruiser was attacked by four American submarines. *Ray* scored two hits, one of which blew off *Kumano's* repaired bow. She was towed into a small port on the western coast of Luzon, where more repairs were started to make her seaworthy. Before these

were completed, however, the ship was attacked by aircraft from the carrier *Ticonderoga*. These quickly placed four bomb hits and five torpedo strikes on the cruiser, which sank inside Santa Cruz harbor.

Mogami class specifications (after second reconstruction into heavy cruisers)	
Displacement:	15,057 tons (full load)
Dimensions:	Length 668ft 6in overall; beam 68ft; draft 36ft
Speed:	35 knots
Range:	7,000–7,500nm at 14 knots
Crew:	58 officers and 838 enlisted personnel (1940)

Tone Class
Design and construction
The naval program and funding which included the two ships that became the *Tone* class were approved in March 1934. Naval General Staff requirements for the two 8,450-ton cruisers in the program were almost identical to those for the *Mogami* class. However, in 1936, while the ships were on the building ways, the requirements were modified. The ships were repurposed as scouting cruisers, which required a larger capacity for seaplanes. Since it was desired that each ship be able to fire her main guns while launching aircraft, the entire main battery was moved forward so as to prevent the possibility of blast damage to the aircraft aft. Once altered, the design called for a ship of 12,500 tons with the ability to carry six to eight seaplanes. Speed was set at 36 knots and radius at 8,000nm at 18 knots.

Much of the design for the *Tone* class was drawn from the *Mogami* class. The general hull lines were the same as on *Mogami* and the bridge was very similar. The propulsion system for the new class was identical to that installed in *Suzuya* and *Kumano*. The four sets of turbines created a total of 152,000shp. On full-power trials, both ships reached speeds of more than 35 knots. Endurance was superior, since fuel capacity was expanded to 2,690 tons. In service, this equated to a range of 12,000nm at 14 knots.

ABOVE LEFT
The first IJN heavy cruiser lost during the war was *Mikuma*, sunk off Midway in June 1942. This iconic shot shows the cruiser in her death throes. The ship was photographed on the afternoon of June 7 by dive-bombers from the carrier *Enterprise*. The results of earlier American attacks are clearly evident. The complete devastation amidships was caused by the explosion of several of the ship's torpedoes. Contrary to myth, the wreckage on No. 4 turret is not that of a US Marine Corps dive-bomber. (Naval History and Heritage Command)

ABOVE RIGHT
Mikuma shown on fire in the June 7 photo sequence taken by *Enterprise* aircraft. Her forward turrets have their guns askew, the result of bomb damage. The first turret has a *hinomaru* painted on top as an aid to friendly air recognition. The mainmast and aircraft deck are entirely gone, the result of an explosion caused by the ship's torpedoes detonating. (Naval History and Heritage Command)

Mogami on June 15, 1944, as she steams with the carriers of the First Mobile Fleet en route to meet the US Navy off the Marianas. For this battle, *Mogami* embarked three Type 0 "Jake" reconnaissance aircraft and two Type 0 "Pete" aircraft. The two carriers to the right are *Shokaku* and *Zuikaku*; *Taiho* is in the center of the picture and a *Hiyo* class carrier is on the left. (Yamato Museum)

ABOVE LEFT

An overhead shot of a *Mogami* class cruiser in February 1943 showing the layout of the five 8in turrets, two of which appear to be painted with air recognition markings. Based on the date, this is probably *Kumano* in the area of Kavieng. (Naval History and Heritage Command)

ABOVE RIGHT

The *Mogami* class cruisers proved to be tough to sink, and this was epitomized by the fate of *Kumano*. On October 26, while retiring from the battle off Samar, she was attacked by aircraft from the carrier *Hancock* in Tablas Strait near the southern tip of Mindoro Island. In this attack, Japanese sources claimed she was hit by three bombs, one seen hitting in this photo. She lost seven of eight boilers, but was able to crawl to temporary safety. (Naval History and Heritage Command)

Tone class construction

Ship	Built at	Laid down	Launched	Commissioned
Tone	Nagasaki by Mitsubishi	12/01/1934	11/21/1937	11/20/1939
Chikuma	Nagasaki by Mitsubishi	10/01/1935	03/19/1938	05/20/1939

This class was the best protected of the IJN's heavy cruisers. The total weight of armor and protective plating was nearly identical to that of the *Mogami* class, but since all the turrets were grouped forward, a heavier scale of protection could be provided over a more compact magazine area. The main belt was sloped at 20 degrees and over the machinery spaces it reached a maximum of 100mm thick, tapering to 65mm. The forward part of the belt that covered the four magazines of the main battery was between 145 and 55mm thick. Overhead protection comprised a middle deck with 31mm over the machinery spaces, increasing to 65mm on the outer portions, while another 56mm of protection was present on the lower deck over the magazines.

Aircraft facilities were designed to carry up to six aircraft, but neither ship ever carried more than five in service. Two catapults were fitted. The aircraft were moved by means of a 79ft crane and a rail system fitted on the ship's deck. No hanger was provided.

Armament

The altered design called for a ship with four triple 6.1in gun turrets, all located forward, five twin 5in guns (the fifth on the centerline aft), four twin 25mm mounts, and two 13mm machine guns in front of the bridge. Unlike on *Mogami*, the *Tone* class was fitted with the more modern Type 94 high-angle director for the 5in guns. A heavy torpedo fit was retained – 12 tubes in triple mounts.

KUMANO UNDER ATTACK BY US CARRIER AIRCRAFT

The saga of *Kumano* during the battle of Leyte Gulf and its aftermath demonstrated the toughness of the IJN's heavy cruisers. After sustaining torpedo and bomb damage during the battle, followed by temporary repairs in Manila, the cruiser attempted to return to Japan. She was attacked on November 6, 1944, by an American wolf pack of four submarines. The four submarines fired a total of 23 torpedoes at *Kumano* and two hit. One blew off the repaired bow and the second hit near the starboard engine room, resulting in all four engine rooms being flooded. *Kumano* was taken under tow and arrived at the small harbor of Santa Cruz on the west coast of Luzon on November 7, 1944. For the next two weeks, the cruiser underwent more repairs to make her seaworthy. This effort was brought to an abrupt halt on November 25, when aircraft from the carrier *Ticonderoga* attacked the tough cruiser and sank her with four 500lb bombs and five torpedoes. This view depicts the immobile cruiser under attack by *Ticonderoga*'s torpedo planes. Twenty-five minutes after being struck by the torpedoes, the cruiser sank with the loss of 441 crewmembers.

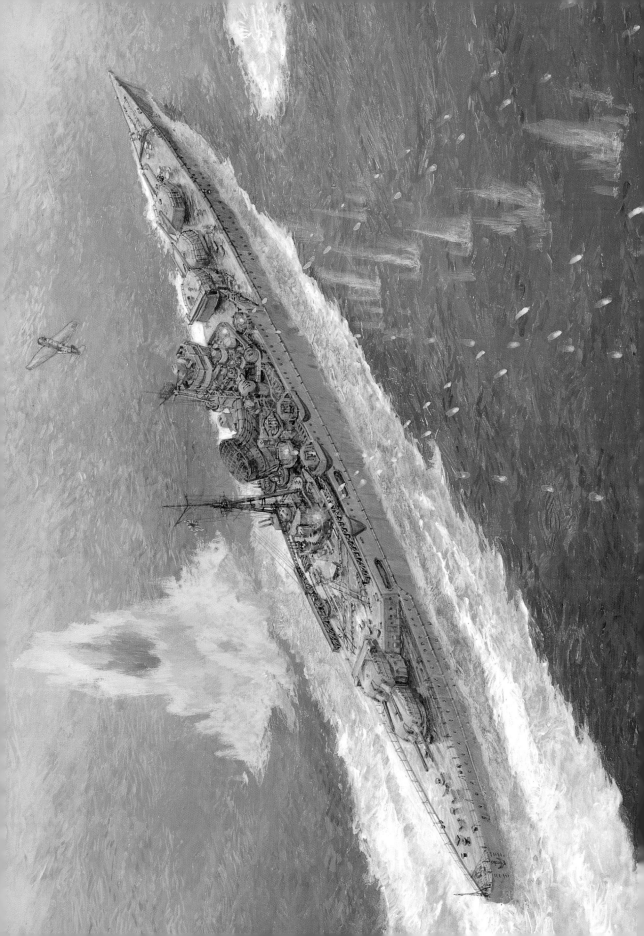

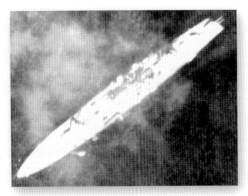

The final chapter in *Kumano's* struggle for survival was played out on November 25, 1944, in Santa Cruz harbor on the western coast of Luzon. The ship is shown here dead in the water following repairs from the November 6 torpedo attack that blew off her bow. The missing bow is clearly evident forward of No. 1 turret. Within minutes of this photo, the ship was struck by four bombs and five torpedoes and finally sunk. (Naval History and Heritage Command)

Before the construction of the ships had proceeded to the upper deck, existing naval treaties lapsed, so the triple 6.1in turrets were replaced with twin 8in turrets. The placement of the turrets did not change, with all four in a pyramid arrangement forward, which meant Nos. 3 and 4 turrets could only fire broadside. The centerline 5in gun mount was deleted before completion, and the 13mm machine-guns were replaced with 25mm guns. A total of 24 torpedoes were carried, 12 in the tubes and another 12 reloads.

Service modifications

After entering service, the *Tone* class proved very satisfactory. They were considered to be the most comfortable of the IJN's cruisers. No modifications were carried out before the war began. After the onset of war, modifications focused on improvements to the radar suite and the light anti-aircraft fit. In February 1943, the ships received a No. 21 radar on the foremast. In June 1944, a No. 13 radar was added to the mainmast and two No. 22 sets were fitted atop the foremast below the No. 21 radar.

Light anti-aircraft guns were added in two phases. In February 1943, two additional twin 25mm mounts were added. In December 1943–January 1944, four triple mounts replaced four of the twin mounts and four single 25mm guns were added, and in June 1944, a further four triple mounts were fitted (two in the area of bridge and two aft) as well as numerous single 25mm mounts.

After returning to Japan following the battle of Leyte Gulf, *Tone* underwent a final series of modifications. By February 1945, four triple mounts were added on the quarterdeck and the number of single 25mm mounts was reduced from 25 to 18. The final number of 25mm barrels embarked was 62. Also, the No. 21 radar, which was considered obsolete, was removed from the foremast and replaced by a No. 22 Modification 4.

Tone class anti-aircraft fit, October 1944				
Ship	Triple mounts	Twin mounts	Single mounts	Total 25mm guns
Tone	8	4	25	57
Chikuma	8	4	13	45]

Wartime service

At the start of the war, the two ships of the class formed *Sentai 8*. The *Tone* class was ideally suited to operate with the IJN's carrier force, since the ships possessed superior endurance and an increased seaplane capacity. The latter was critical, as Japanese carrier doctrine placed much of the responsibility for scouting on the seaplanes of the escorting battleships and cruisers, thus allowing the maximum number of carrier aircraft to be retained for offensive operations. In November 1941, *Sentai 8* was assigned to the Striking Force (*Kido Butai*), where it remained until after the battle of Midway.

Both ships accompanied the Japanese carriers on the raids on Pearl Harbor and Wake Island in December 1941; on Rabaul, Kavieng, Lae, and Salamaua in January 1942; and on Port Darwin in February 1942. In late February/early March, the *Kido Butai* operated south of Java, and *Tone* and *Chikuma* used gunfire to sink a merchant ship and an American destroyer. This was followed by the Indian Ocean raid, in which seaplanes from *Sentai*

8 performed scouting duties and sighted two British heavy cruisers, which were sunk by air attack. The two ships then returned to Japan in April.

In June 1942, *Sentai 8* remained attached to the *Kido Butai* and played key roles in the Midway operation. It was an aircraft from *Tone* that first spotted the American carrier force, but issued frustratingly vague contact reports. By the time the aircraft reported the actual presence of carriers, a train of events had been set in place that resulted in the destruction of four of the IJN's fleet carriers, the turning point of the Pacific War. During the battle, *Sentai 8* was attacked several times by American carrier aircraft, but suffered no damage.

During the Guadalcanal campaign, *Sentai 8* still operated with the IJN's reformed carrier force. Both cruisers were active during the carrier battle of the Eastern Solomons in August 1942 and the final carrier battle of 1942 at Santa Cruz. During this battle, *Chikuma* suffered moderate damage on October 26 when she was hit by bombs dropped by dive-bombers from the carrier *Hornet*. Two bombs struck the bridge, then a near miss flooded two boiler rooms, and finally a bomb hit the starboard forward torpedo room. Fortunately for the Japanese, the ship's torpedoes had been jettisoned only minutes before, so the damage was contained. However, *Chikuma* suffered a heavy loss of life (151 dead and 165 wounded) and repairs were not completed until late February 1943.

Chikuma was part of the ill-fated move of a number of cruisers to Rabaul in November 1943. During the American carrier air attack, she suffered only near misses with no damage. *Sentai 8* was then held in readiness for most of 1944, as were the Imperial Navy's other heavy cruisers. On March 2, 1944, however, the two ships deployed into the Indian Ocean to conduct commerce raiding. *Tone* sank a British merchant vessel and took 108 crew and passengers onboard. Of these, 72 were beheaded on *Tone* during the night of March 18–19.

The next operation for *Sentai 8* was the battle of the Philippine Sea, from which both cruisers emerged undamaged. For the IJN's last desperate attempt to engage the US Navy decisively at Leyte Gulf, *Sentai 8* was disbanded and *Tone* and *Chikuma* were assigned to *Sentai 7* with *Suzuya* and *Kumano*. As part of the First Diversionary Attack Force, *Tone* and *Chikuma* participated in the sinking of the escort carrier *Gambier Bay* off Samar on October 25. The American escort carrier force exacted revenge when an air-launched torpedo hit *Chikuma* amidships, flooding the engine rooms and bringing the

This fine view of *Tone*, taken in early 1942, shows the layout of her class of ships, with her forward main armament and aircraft facilities aft. Note the large crane for handling aircraft. Four aircraft are embarked, including three Type 0 "Jake" reconnaissance seaplanes and a Type 95 "Dave" used to spot for the ship's guns. (*Ships of the World* magazine)

An overhead view of *Tone* in 1941, which clearly shows the layout of the ship's secondary and anti-aircraft armament as well as her aircraft-handling facilities. The six 25mm twin mounts can be seen in pairs in front of the bridge, abaft the smokestack, and near the mainmast. This view clearly shows the system of deck-mounted rails and turntables used to move the floatplanes on deck. (Yamato Museum)

ship to a stop. Repairs were unsuccessful, so when the Japanese withdrew, orders were given to scuttle the ship. Her crew was taken off, and she was sunk by torpedo. That night, the destroyer that had rescued *Chikuma's* crew was sunk; only a single member from *Chikuma's* crew survived.

Tone emerged from Leyte Gulf with moderate damage. She was hit by three bombs in the Sibuyan Sea on October 24 and during the battle off Samar, she was struck by a single 5in shell. While withdrawing from the engagement, she was hit by another bomb from an aircraft from the escort carrier *Kitkun Bay*, but was able to retire without further damage.

After returning to Japan and undergoing a refit, *Tone* was moored near Etajima, intended to be used as a training ship at the IJN's Naval Academy. A series of American carrier raids, however, hunted *Tone* to extinction. The first on March 19, 1945, resulted in only light damage. A much larger raid on July 24 placed three bomb hits on *Tone* and delivered at least seven near misses. These caused severe flooding and the ship began to settle by the stern. A further attack on July 28 added a rocket hit. The ship was abandoned for good on August 5 and was scrapped in 1948, the last of the IJN's cruisers to disappear.

Chikuma at high speed under air attack on October 26, 1942, during the battle of Santa Cruz. The smoke in the area of the bridge is the result of fires caused by two bomb hits inflicted seconds before. Note the four turrets trained to port and the *hinomaru* painted on turret No. 2. (Naval History and Heritage Command)

Tone class specifications	
Displacement:	15,239 tons (full load)
Dimensions:	Length 661ft 4in overall; beam 63ft 8in; draft 35ft 9in
Speed:	35 knots
Range	12,000nm at 14 knots
Crew:	59 officers and 815 enlisted personnel as designed

ANALYSIS AND CONCLUSION

Japanese heavy cruiser designers provided the IJN with a series of fast, well-armed and tough ships. The Japanese consistently emphasized offensive capabilities in their heavy cruisers, and this gave their navy a large number of formidable platforms. Yet while the Japanese succeeded in producing fearsome-looking cruisers with heavy armament that tended to overshadow their American and British rivals, Japanese cruiser designs were not as well balanced as the later American treaty cruiser designs. Given their focus on offensive capabilities, Japanese heavy cruisers suffered from a lack of adequate armored protection.

G

THE *TONE* CLASS

This shows *Tone* in June 1942 in her early war configuration at the battle of Midway. The unique appearance of the ship is evident, with all 8in turrets placed forward of the bridge and the rear of the ship devoted to aircraft handling. These ships never carried more than five aircraft. A typical early war mix was three Type 0 reconnaissance seaplanes and two Navy Type 95 reconnaissance seaplanes (Allied codename "Dave") used primarily for spotting. Of note, though, at the battle of Midway, *Tone* only embarked four aircraft (two Type 0 and two Type 95). The appearance of the ship's bridge and smokestack is clearly based on the *Mogami* design.

One of the two principal Japanese heavy cruiser floatplanes in service at the start of the war was the Navy Type 94 reconnaissance seaplane (E7N2, perhaps best known by its Allied codename "Alf"). The Type 94 (shown right) was the standard catapult-launched long-range seaplane in service until 1942 when it was replaced by the Navy Type 0 reconnaissance seaplane (E13A1) which was given the Allied codename "Jake" (shown left). This aircraft possessed good performance and served through the end of the war with over 1,300 built.

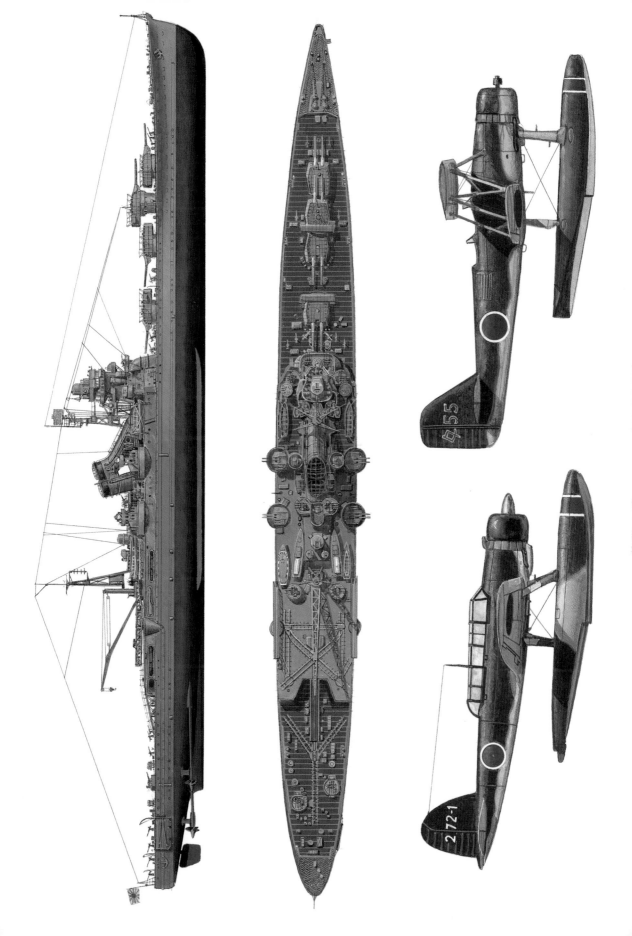

The persistent issue of overweight designs resulted in several undesirable consequences. Instability was a problem that reached its zenith in the design of the *Mogami* class, which required a wholesale reconstruction to rectify. Additional weight also reduced endurance and freeboard; the latter condition had the effect of pushing more of the main armor belt below the waterline, which increased the potential for damage from enemy shellfire. For all cruiser designs, underwater protection was inadequate, since the Japanese themselves had calculated that their passive torpedo defenses could only withstand 440lb of high explosive. Since the standard American air-launched torpedo during the war contained a warhead with 600lb of Torpex (50 percent more powerful than TNT), and the Mark 14 submarine-launched torpedo had a Torpex warhead with 643lb, Japanese cruisers were obviously vulnerable to torpedo damage.

The principal design difference between Japanese cruisers and American cruisers was the inclusion of a heavy torpedo armament. As predicted by some Japanese designers, inclusion of torpedoes proved to be a double-edged sword. As has been recounted, use of cruiser-fired torpedoes was decisive in several instances, namely during the battles of Java Sea and Savo Island. However, the loss of three cruisers (*Mikuma*, *Furutaka*, *Suzuya*) was directly attributable to detonations of on-board torpedoes and two other cruisers (*Aoba* and *Mogami*) were severely damaged in the same way.

During the course of the war, the Imperial Navy's cruisers proved increasingly vulnerable to air attack, although this was not in itself due to a design flaw. Indeed, the primary cause for the destruction of the majority of the IJN's heavy cruisers was air attack (see data box). The Japanese were not unaware of this vulnerability, but the continuing addition of growing numbers of light anti-aircraft guns on the ships did nothing to lessen their vulnerability. The lack of a medium anti-aircraft gun, like the 40mm Bofors used by the US Navy, cost the Japanese dearly, as the inadequate 25mm gun combined with poor fire control essentially resulted in the destruction of the Japanese heavy cruiser force.

Losses of IJN heavy cruisers by primary cause	
Due to surface attack:	(2) *Furutaka, Haguro*
Due to submarine attack:	(4) *Kako, Ashigara, Atago, Maya*
Due to air attack:	(10) *Aoba, Kinugasa, Nachi, Chokai, Mikuma, Kumano, Suzuya, Mogami, Tone, Chikuma*

Nevertheless, heavy cruisers must be seen as one of the IJN's success stories. These ships spearheaded Japanese expansion into the critical Dutch East Indies, shattering all Allied opposition. Japanese heavy cruisers served with distinction during the Guadalcanal campaign, marked by the victory at Savo Island. By the end of the war, all but two had been sunk as the Americans exploited Japanese weaknesses in anti-aircraft and anti-submarine warfare, but the fighting record of the IJN's heavy cruiser force was unmatched by any other navy during World War II.

BIBLIOGRAPHY

Backer, Steve, *Japanese Heavy Cruisers*, Chatham Publishing, London (2006)

Campbell, John, *Naval Weapons of World War Two*, Naval Institute Press, Annapolis, Maryland (1985)

Evans, David C. and Mark R. Peattie, *Kaigun: Strategy, Tactics and Technology in the Imperial Japanese Navy 1887–1941*, Naval Institute Press, Annapolis, Maryland (1997)

Goralski, Waldemar and Slawomir Lipiecki, *Japanese Heavy Cruiser Takao*, Kagero, Lublin, Poland (2007)

Goralski, Waldemar and Miroslaw Skwiot, *Heavy Cruiser Aoba*, Kagero, Lublin, Poland (2008)

Jentschura, Hansgeorg, and Dieter Jung and Peter Mickel, *Warships of the Imperial Japanese Navy 1869–1945*, Naval Institute Press, Annapolis, Maryland (1977)

Lacroix, Eric and Linton Wells II, *Japanese Cruisers of the Pacific War*, Naval Institute Press, Annapolis, Maryland (1997)

Marriot, Leo, *Treaty Cruisers*, Pen and Sword Maritime, Barnsley (2005)

O'Hara, Vincent P., *The US Navy Against the Axis*, Naval Institute Press, Annapolis, Maryland (2006)

Patton, Wayne, *Japanese Heavy Cruisers of World War II in Action*, Squadron/Signal Publications, Carrollton, Texas, n.d.

Skulski, Janusz, *The Heavy Cruiser Takao*, Naval Institute Press, Annapolis, Maryland (1994)

Stille, Mark, *USN Cruiser vs IJN Cruiser*, Osprey, Oxford (2009)

Watts, Anthony J. and Brian G. Gordon, *The Imperial Japanese Navy*, Macdonald, London (1971)

Whitley, M. J., *Cruisers of World War Two*, Naval Institute Press, Annapolis, Maryland (1995)

Wiper, Steve, *IJN Myoko Class Heavy Cruiser*, Classic Warships Publishing, Tucson, Arizona (2002)

Wiper, Steve, *IJN Takao Class Heavy Cruiser*, Classic Warships Publishing, Tucson, Arizona (2008)

For an online reference to the ships of the Imperial Japanese Navy, see www.combinedfleet.com

Aoba sunk in shallow water just south of Kure Naval Yard, shown in October 1945. Not visible in the view is her missing stern. Her light anti-aircraft guns have been removed, but the No. 21 radar remains on her foremast. (Author's collection)

INDEX

Note: letters in **bold** refer to plates and illustrations.